C0-ATV-951

Passing On the Torch

Passing On the Torch

How to Convey Religious Values to Young People

Roger L. Dudley

REVIEW AND HERALD PUBLISHING ASSOCIATION
Washington, DC 20039-0555
Hagerstown, MD 21740

Copyright © 1986 by Review and Herald Publishing Association
Editor: Raymond H. Woolsey
Book design: Richard Steadham

Printed in U.S.A.

The author assumes full responsibility for the accuracy of all facts and quotations as cited in this book.

Unless otherwise noted, all Bible quotations in this book are from the *Holy Bible, New International Version.* Copyright © 1973, 1978, International Bible Society. Used by permission of Zondervan Bible Publishers.

Library of Congress Cataloging in Publication Data

Dudley, Roger L.
  Passing on the torch.
  Bibliography: p. 186.
  1. Youth—Conduct of life. 2. Youth—religious life. 3. Values. 4. Moral education. I. Title.
BJ1661.D83 1986   207   86-10044

ISBN 0-8280-0348-3

Contents

Introduction

Parents and religious leaders are rightly concerned that the youthful generation will come to cherish the values that they themselves have found so important, and will eventually make these values their own. The concern is not a recent one. Stephen Wieting reminds us that:

"A recurrent focus of social philosophy since Plato's *Republic* has been the threat to society posed by the possibility that the young might not adopt the essential wisdom and values of that society. . . . A concern with generational issues is easy to understand. If a society is to continue its existence beyond one generation, the members must transmit what they consider to be necessary knowledge and values. The continuity of a social system by definition requires transmission between generations." [1]

Go back further. A thousand years before Plato the transmission of values was of concern to the people of God. As the Israelites were about to cross the Jordan River into the Promised Land, Joshua selected twelve men and instructed them: "Go over before the ark of the Lord your God into the middle of the Jordan. Each of you is to take up a stone on his shoulder . . . to serve as a sign among you. In the future, when your children ask you, 'What do these stones mean?' tell them that the flow of the Jordan was cut off before the ark of the covenant of the Lord. When it crossed the Jordan, the waters of the Jordan were cut off. These stones are to be a memorial to the people of Israel forever" (Joshua 4:5-7).

We also read the sad account of the failure to pass

religious values along in such a way that the younger generation would claim them as their own. The people of Israel did serve the Lord "throughout the lifetime of Joshua and of the elders who outlived him." But "after that whole generation had been gathered to their fathers, another generation grew up, who knew neither the Lord nor what he had done for Israel. Then the Israelites did evil in the eyes of the Lord and served the Baals. They forsook the Lord, the God of their fathers, who had brought them out of Egypt. They followed and worshiped various gods of the peoples around them. They provoked the Lord to anger" (Judges 2:7,10-12).

What can *we* do today—we who compose the generation poised on the borders of the antitypical Land of Promise—to prevent that fate from happening to us and our children? What can we do that will help our youth to cherish the best of our spiritual values? I have been vitally interested in this subject for a number of years. Ever since completing my earlier work, *Why Teenagers Reject Religion and What to Do About It,* I have been searching for solutions to the elusive problem of how to transmit religious values. This book is my opportunity to share the results of my search.

The presentation is divided into three sections. Section One, "Understanding Values," looks at what values are and why we are suffering a value shortage today. It especially considers the meaning of religion and religious values and attempts to describe the kind of values we should seek to transmit. Finally, it examines the process of obtaining values and the criteria by which values may be judged. While some practical helps are implicit in the material, this may be considered the theoretical or philosophical part. I believe it to be essential background for putting into operation the strategies that are subsequently described. This section occupies chapters 1 through 8.

Section Two, "How Values Are Acquired," looks at several of the historic scientific explanations as to how moral development occurs. It also examines some of the most representative research on values transmission from both the past and the present. Finally, it reports on an original piece of research among a national sample of Seventh-day Adventist families. This section might be called the scientific or technical part. Some readers may wish to skip it and move immediately into the practical, but it provides the reason for what follows. Therefore, readers who wish to know why they do what they do will find it invaluable. It comprises chapters 9 through 15.

The final section, "How to Teach Values," is the practical, or "how to," part. It presents many strategies, methods, and techniques that can be used to facilitate values development both in the home and in the classroom. Furthermore, these ideas have been described in terms of *religious* values. These suggestions will be found in chapters 16 through 21.

And so we begin this journey together, filled with solemnity as we sense its importance. We are not talking about trivial things. "Character building," urges Ellen White, "is the most important work ever entrusted to human beings; and never before was its diligent study so important as now. Never was any previous generation called to meet issues so momentous; never before were young men and young women confronted by perils so great as confront them today." [2]

With a full realization of the magnitude of the issues before us, shall we explore together? Let us implore our heavenly Father for wisdom and invite Him to be our guide.

Roger L. Dudley

Notes

[1] Stephen G. Wieting, "An Examination of Intergenerational Patterns of Religious Belief and Practice," *Sociological Analysis* 36 (Summer, 1975): 137.
[2] Ellen G. White, *Education* (Mountain View, Calif.: Pacific Press Pub. Assn., 1952), p. 225.

Understanding Values

CHAPTER 1

Prices, Priorities, and Preferences

Recently a 12-year-old girl with a cancerous tumor refused chemotherapy on religious grounds even though physicians warned that she faced certain death unless treatment was begun immediately. A 17-year-old girl on her first date succumbed to the sexual advances of her partner when he pressed her with "Don't you *want* me to love you?" A preadolescent boy spent months collecting aluminum cans for recycling in order to raise money to purchase a clothes washer for a family in poverty. A teenager who had promised his parents that he would not get involved in drugs joined in a "pot" party because all his friends were doing it and he "didn't want to be different." A young man trained vigorously—eight to ten hours a day—for months, sacrificing most of his social life, in the hope of making the U.S. Olympic team and maybe even winning a gold medal.

What do these five cases have in common? All made decisions that would be important in determining the course of their lives, and all made those decisions on the basis of a set of values. The first girl valued her religious convictions and the approval of her parents and fellow church members more than life itself. The second young woman valued being wanted and cared for more than safety from undesirable consequences that might result from her hasty decision. The first boy valued the good feeling that comes from unselfish behavior in helping others more than the things he could have purchased for himself with the money or the activities he could have pursued with the time that he invested. The second young man valued the approval of his peers more than his promise to his parents or the possible damage to his health that might occur. The Olympic hopeful valued the sense of achievement and the glory of public esteem more than comfort and a more normal social schedule.

Some of these youth may have consciously consulted their values before making the decision. Others may not have given them a thought and were unaware of how their basic values shaped the decision-making process. But consciously considered or not, values were a key antecedent of their behavior. So they are with each of us.

Valuing

The noun *value* means "something of worth." It indicates those beliefs, attitudes, behaviors, objects, et cetera, that we believe to be important or that we place worth on, particularly when we must choose between them and some alternatives.

But the word *value* means not only a *product* (what we value) but also a *process* (the method by which we arrive at what we value). This process begins in early childhood and continues throughout our entire lives. We are constantly assigning relative worth to things or concepts such as wealth, beauty, power, popularity, happiness, altruism, achievement, freedom, security, adventure, peace of mind, and salvation. We do this not in abstract terms but as these values are called into action in the situations that arise in the course of everyday living.

The Bible contains many value statements. Let us consider a few of the more prominent ones. Abraham obeyed God, turned his back on the city of Ur, and traveled to the Promised Land, "for he was looking forward to the city with foundations, whose architect and builder is God" (Heb. 11:10). By faith Moses "chose to be mistreated along with the people of God rather than to enjoy the pleasures of sin for a short time. He regarded disgrace for the sake of Christ as of greater value than the treasures of Egypt, because he was looking ahead to his reward" (verses 25, 26). Both Abraham and Moses gave up something valuable in order to gain something they considered even more valuable.

As Joshua gave his final charge to the people he had led into the Promised Land, he exhorted them: "Choose for yourselves this day whom you will serve. . . . But as for me and my household, we will serve the Lord" (Joshua 24:15). Making important choices always calls values into action.

Jesus encouraged His followers: "So do not worry, saying, 'What shall we eat?' or 'What shall we drink?' or 'What shall we wear?' For . . . your heavenly Father knows that you need them. But seek first his kingdom and his righteousness, and all these things will be given to you as well" (Matt. 6:31-33). Spiritual realities are seen to be of more value than temporal necessities and, indeed, even to encompass them.

Perhaps one of the clearest of all biblical statements is the counsel of Jesus: "Whoever wants to save his life [or soul] will lose it, but whoever loses his life for me will find it. What good will it be for a man if he gains the whole world, yet forfeits his soul? Or what can a man give in exchange for his soul?" (chap. 16:25, 26). Since the Bible concerns itself with the great issues of life, it must deal heavily in values.

A Closer Look at Values

With this brief background we now turn to a closer examination of the nature of values and the process by which they are acquired. Merton Strommen, a well-known youth researcher, offers this definition: "Values are ideas people have about the 'good life' and about what life means. They are the ideas we use to tell whether we like something or not; whether it is important or unimportant to us; whether we are frightened of or feel good about an object, an event, a course of action, or a person." [1]

"We hold that all values come from the one fundamental idea: good and evil. . . . Our concept of good and evil is the basis we use to rank everything else, including all other values, beliefs, abstract ideas like truth, scientific theories, people, even God. Of course, nothing human is ever *all* good or *all* evil. There are mixtures of good and evil. Values are how we grasp the mixture of good and evil in any combination of circumstances involving interaction between ourselves and external reality." [2]

This definition helps us to see values as not simply a matter of taste or custom (which some are) but to recognize that, fundamentally, values involve *moral* dimensions. From another viewpoint, Jack Fraenkel observes: "A value is an idea—a concept—about what someone thinks is important in life. When a person values something, he or she deems it worthwhile—worth having, worth doing, or worth trying to obtain. . . . *Ethics* refers to the study and justification of conduct—how people behave. At the base of the study of ethics is the question of morals—the reflective consideration of what is right and wrong." [3]

Values refer, then, not only to mental concepts and judgments but to behavior; not only to talk but to action. The mention of ethics involves us with one of the oldest fields of human endeavor—the study of philosophy. This reminds us that the weighing of values has been going on in every age and every culture since the day that Eve decided to eat the fruit of the forbidden tree, supposing that the advantages to be gained outweighed the consequences against which God had warned (see Gen. 3:1-19). George Knight, a professor of educational philosophy in a Christian university explains: "Axiology is the branch of philosophy that seeks to answer the question: 'What is of value?'. . . Man desires some things more than others—he has preferences. . . . Value systems are not universally agreed upon . . . because axiological systems are built upon conceptions of reality and truth." [4]

Knight goes on to differentiate between "conceived values" (those that people verbalize but may not actualize) and "operative values" (those they act upon). He notes that axiology has two main branches—ethics and aesthetics.

This book will concern itself only with the ethical branch, which is defined as "the study of moral values and conduct. It seeks to answer such questions as 'What should I do?' 'What is the good life for all people?' and 'What is good conduct?' " [5]

Some of the timeless questions raised in the study of ethics are (1) "Are ethical standards and moral values absolute or relative?" (2) "Do universal moral values exist?" (3) "Does the end ever justify the means?" (4) "Can morality be separated from religion?" (5) "Who or what forms the basis of ethical authority?" [6]

So then, values involve moral judgments and ethical behavior. But there is still more. They also encompass feelings. Fraenkel points out that "a value is a powerful emotional commitment, a strong liking for something." [7]

Value Indicators

What are the values that a person holds most dear? We cannot find out by X-raying the head—or the heart. We cannot attach an arm cuff like that for a blood-pressure-measuring device and obtain a digital readout. Fraenkel observes: "Values cannot be seen directly; they must be inferred from value indicators—what people say and do. Both the actions and statements of people offer clues about their values." [8]

"What people say!" While people may claim one thing and do another, the trend of their everyday, unguarded conversation must inevitably reveal their underlying values. "Words . . . which indicate or imply that an individual or group considers a particular thing or group of things to have a certain amount of worth, merit, or quality . . . are called *value judgments*." [9] We will be paying a great deal of attention to value judgments in this book.

Actions, however, provide the most fertile field for inferring a person's values. What does he or she do with spare time when not coaxed or threatened into doing what someone else believes is important? What does one choose to buy or not to buy with discretionary funds? If a young man spends his time playing arcade games, does not prepare his lessons, and fails his coursework, what does that say about his values? What about a high school graduate who goes to work in order to make payments on a sporty car rather than continue with a college education?

Consider the values revealed in this Associated Press dispatch filed at Oakland, California, May 16, 1950: "A father gave his life to save his son's here today, following a blood exchange operation. The son, 11-year-old Robert Bruce Lawrence, probably will recover, physicians said. He has nephrosis, a kidney disease, and needed a complete change of blood. Sidney E. Lawrence, 40, the father, volunteered for the operation. The bloods were of matching type. He was told that in such an operation, there always is some danger to the donor because of foreign material he is taking into his own system. 'Go ahead,' he said. The three-hour operation was performed several days ago. Today the father died."

Or what values do you see operating in this account taken from a personal letter to me, dated December 12, 1968, from R. B. Caldwell, then assistant treasurer of the General Conference of Seventh-day Adventists?

"Recently six of our Adventist young men in western Cuba were told that they must give up their belief in the Sabbath or forfeit their lives before a firing squad. They remained firm and the following morning were lined up for execution. As the six men were standing there, some were praying; others were singing. Slowly the command was given to fire. As the guns were fired no soldiers fell, however, because the guns were loaded with blank cartridges rather than bullets. The Adventists were instructed to return to their homes, not to bother the government, and the government would not bother them."

Often our values are rather vague—not sorted out or clearly defined. It is in value-conflict situations that we are forced to choose what is really worthwhile to us. We want to help our fellow student who is having difficulty preparing for the examination, but the teacher grades "on the curve." We have been reared with standards of purity and self-respect, but we don't want to be passed by in the popularity contest. We prize honesty, but we really need the extra cash that fudging on our expense account could bring. How can we best help our youth to develop and articulate truly worthwhile values? This book will attempt to answer this question.

Our values determine all of life's significant choices—our response to the claims of God, our choice of career, our selection of a marriage partner, how we spend our money, our use of leisure time, and on and on. If youth learn to value wisely, they will find that the process develops mature, principled adults.

Notes

[1] Merton P. Strommen, Milo L. Brekke, Ralph Underwager, and Arthur L. Johnson, *A Study of Generations* (Minneapolis: Augsburg Publishing House, 1972), p. 78.

[2] *Ibid.*, p. 79.

[3] Jack R. Fraenkel, *How to Teach About Values* (Englewood Cliffs, N.J.: Prentice-Hall, 1977), pp. 6, 7.

[4] George R. Knight, *Philosophy and Education* (Berrien Springs, Mich.: Andrews University Press, 1980), p. 28.

[5] *Ibid.*, p. 29.

[6] *Ibid.*, p. 30.

[7] Fraenkel, *op. cit.*, pp. 10, 11.

[8] *Ibid.*, p. 16.

[9] *Ibid.*, p. 23.

CHAPTER 2

Beliefs, Attitudes, and Values

Suppose a man believes that there is a God and that He sent His Son, Jesus, to be the Saviour of the world. Would you say that Christianity is a value for him? Maybe. But maybe not. The Bible asks and answers the question this way: "You believe that there is one God. Good! Even the demons believe that—and shudder" (James 2:19).

Well, what if a person has a positive attitude toward something—say, respect for law and civic responsibility? Does that constitute a value? Possibly. But we might note that a former Vice President of the United States, who was one of the most outspoken champions of law and order, was forced to resign his office in the wake of a scandal over falsifying personal income tax returns. And Pilate was favorably disposed toward Jesus: "Look, I am bringing him out to you to let you know that I find no basis for a charge against him" (John 19:4). But we could hardly call Jesus a value in Pilate's life.

How about actions? A woman volunteers time for social welfare work to assist the needy. Surely this is a value for her. Even here caution is called for. The apostle Paul challenges us to look at our motives critically; he writes: "If I give all I possess to the poor and surrender my body to the flames, but have not love, I gain nothing" (1 Cor. 13:3).

Recently I heard about a man who was not a believer in God but who was married to a devout Christian. He respected both her beliefs and her desire to rear their children in her faith. So he accompanied her to weekly church services and even participated in family worship, reading Bible stories to the children. He did all this while personally being an atheist!

Important Interrelationships

In this chapter I propose to examine the relationships among attitudes, beliefs, behaviors, and values. In so doing, I will draw on the work done by Milton Rokeach, psychologist and one of America's foremost authorities in the field of values. Let us begin with attitudes. Milton Rokeach offers this definition: "An attitude is a relatively enduring organization of beliefs around an object or situation predisposing one to respond in some preferential manner." [1]

"A belief," Rokeach continues, "is any simple proposition, conscious or unconscious, inferred from what a person says or does, capable of being preceded by the phrase 'I believe that . . .' " [2] Beliefs may be categorized under three headings. A *descriptive* belief expresses a supposed fact that can be verified as true or false (I believe that the sun rises in the east). An *evaluative* belief states what one considers to be desirable or undesirable (I believe this ice cream is good). It cannot be verified as true or false since it is rooted in personal experience. A *prescriptive* or *exhortatory* belief states what one believes the situation should be (I believe children should obey their parents). It too is personal and cannot be verified. Each belief contains a cognitive, an affective, and a behavioral component, and "all beliefs are predispositions to action." [3]

Having explained attitudes and beliefs, Rokeach offers a definition of a value. It differs somewhat from those set forth in the previous chapter because the frame of reference is the relationship between beliefs and values. According to Rokeach, a value is "a type of belief, centrally located within one's total belief system, about how one ought or ought not to behave, or about some end-state of existence worth or not worth attaining. Values are thus abstract ideals, positive or negative, not tied to any specific object or situation, representing a person's beliefs about ideal modes of conduct and ideal terminal goals." [4]

In another work Rokeach explains that values are more fundamental than attitudes because a person's values determine his or her attitudes as well as behavior.[5] A person may well have thousands of attitudes, yet only several dozens of values. Notice that Rokeach has identified two types of values. A *terminal* value refers to a desired end-state of existence, while an *instrumental* value refers to a desired mode of behavior. He has proposed eighteen of each type. Rokeach concludes that "a *value system* is a hierarchical organization—a rank ordering—of ideals or values in terms of importance." [6] This rank ordering is fundamental to his system of value education.

Rokeach believes that a basic harmony must exist between attitude and behavior within the value system. "If a person acts contrary to one attitude, it must mean that he acted in accord with a second (or third or fourth) attitude that overrode the first attitude in importance." [7] This suggests that tracing behavior back to attitude is a complex process. Further, "since an attitude object must always be encountered within some situation about which we also have an attitude, a minimum condition for social behavior is the activation of at least two interacting attitudes, one concerning the attitude object and the other concerning the situation." [8]

How Values Operate

It is interesting to try to trace the outworking of intertwined values in the life of someone such as Mohandas Gandhi. It seems evident that high on Gandhi's list of terminal values were the equality of all people, freedom and independence, and a world at peace. On the other hand, he had little regard for values such as wealth, pleasure, and a comfortable life. His most important instrumental values were probably nonviolence and courage. The situation in which these values found focus was the struggle for Indian independence from Great Britain, and the caste system which divided India and made the lives of millions an intolerable burden.

The results of this interaction between the values of this remarkable man and his contemporary situation are well known. Gandhi renounced all personal comforts and identified himself with the Untouchable class. He captured the imagination of his countrymen and became the soul and voice of India. He gained permission for Untouchables to enter sacred Hindu temples that had been off-limits to them for hundreds of years. He led his nation in nonviolent protest against British rule. He taught his people to accept without complaint whatever suffering the exercise of their convictions brought upon them. He saw his patient, painstaking methods finally force the mighty British Empire to grant India independence. He was killed by an Indian zealot impatient with his methodology.

Rokeach explains: "To say that a person 'has a value' is to say that he has an enduring belief that a specific mode of conduct or end-state of existence is personally and socially preferable to alternative modes of conduct or end-states of existence. Once a value is internalized it becomes, consciously or unconsciously, a standard or criterion for guiding action, for developing and maintaining attitudes toward relevant objects and situations, for justifying one's own and other's actions and attitudes, for morally judging self and others, and for comparing self with others. Finally, a value is a standard employed to influence the values, attitudes, and actions of at least some others—our children's, for example." [9]

Most people will affirm traditional values such as peace, honesty, fidelity in marriage, equality of persons, and altruism. After all, who wants to be against motherhood, apple pie, and the flag? But the rub comes when these good values are mutually exclusive. We are often confronted with situations where we cannot behave in a manner congruent with all our values. They are in conflict. In a given situation we may not be able to be both compassionate and competent or truthful and patriotic. We may be forced to prioritize our values and choose between them. Teaching our youth the rules for making these choices and resolving these conflicts lies at the very heart of value transmission between the generations. It will be our major concern throughout these pages.

An Experimental Modification of Values

Psychologists have discovered that to effect change in a person's attitudes and values, a state of imbalance or inconsistency must exist. Rokeach conducted an experiment in which he exposed a group of Michigan State University students to information that made them consciously aware of inconsistencies within their own value and attitude systems, inconsistencies of which they had not been previously aware.[10]

The students were asked to rank the eighteen terminal values. As defined by Rokeach, they are a comfortable life, an exciting life, a sense of accomplishment, a world at peace, a world of beauty, equality, family security, freedom, happiness, inner harmony, mature love, national security, pleasure, salvation, self-respect, social recognition, true friendship, and wisdom.

The students ranked *freedom* high (first of eighteen) and *equality* as eleventh. The experimenter then confronted the students with this evidence and other answers on their questionnaires that seemed to support the fact that they were interested in their own freedom but did not care a great deal about the freedom of other people. Subsequent tests given three weeks, five months, and seventeen months later revealed that the students were becoming aware of the inconsistencies in their value system and that they were dissatisfied with their initial ranking of the eighteen terminal values.

Rokeach found it sobering that a psychologist could produce such long-lasting changes in values, attitudes, and behavior following such brief experimental treatment. The ethical implications demand that much thought should go into proper safeguards to protect the rights and dignity of individuals who are subjected to attempts to modify their values. But the cheering news from this experiment is that parents and other youth leaders may be optimistic about the prospects for transmitting their own values to the next generation, if proper methods are used.

Notes

[1] Milton Rokeach, *Beliefs, Attitudes, and Values* (San Francisco: Jossey-Bass, Inc., 1968), p. 112.

[2] *Ibid.*, p. 113.

[3] *Ibid.*

[4] *Ibid.*, p. 124.

[5] ———, "Long-Range Experimental Modification of Values, Attitudes, and Behavior," *American Psychologist* 26 (May, 1971): 453-457.

[6] ———, *Beliefs, Attitudes, and Values*, p. 124.

[7] *Ibid.*, p. 128.

[8] *Ibid.*, p. 132.

[9] *Ibid.*, pp. 159, 160.

[10] ———, "Long-Range Experimental Modification of Values, Attitudes, and Behaviors," *American Psychologist, loc. cit.*

CHAPTER 3

Crisis in the Value Mart

The American national conscience was deeply troubled a few years ago when Kitty Genovese was stabbed to death outside her apartment in New York City at 3:00 A.M. What made the incident so horrifying was that Kitty fought off her attacker for thirty minutes—all the while screaming for help. And she was heard. Later investigation revealed that about forty neighbors came to their windows during the ordeal. Some shouted at the murderer to leave his victim alone. But not one came to her assistance or even called the police. Each was waiting for someone else to take action.

And consider Eleanor Bradley, who tripped and fell on Fifth Avenue in New York and suffered a broken leg. She lay helpless on the sidewalk for forty minutes while hundreds of passersby kept on walking.

In reviewing research on these and similar cases, Elliot Aronson concluded that a victim is less likely to get help if a large number of people are watching his or her distress.[1] Thus, nonintervention can be viewed as *an act of conformity*. "If nobody else is doing anything, it must not be appropriate to do so." People tend to take their cues from the people around them.

It is precisely this lack of ability to think and act for oneself on the basis of a set of personal principles that epitomizes a value crisis in contemporary society. Today a pervasive sense of loss exists—an uneasy feeling that old-fashioned moral virtues have eroded. We see a growing lack of trust in leaders in government, business, the judicial system, and even the church. Can anyone be trusted to do right because it is right?

Perhaps the most vivid illustration of this moral malaise is the so-called Watergate crisis of 1972-1974. American citizens saw their President and his advisers misuse power, tender bribes, pervert the legal system, and repeatedly lie to the public in an attempt to cover up their actions.

Of course, Watergate is only one sample of the crisis in the value mart. Lieutenant William Calley, who was convicted of the deliberate and unprovoked murder of women and children at My Lai during the Vietnam War, freely admitted to these acts but said that he felt that this was justifiable obedience to the authority of his superior officers. Other examples could be cited to support the contention that the current crisis in values exists because of the lack of principled people who cannot be swayed by the influence of those around them. .

In our modern world, technological advance has been seen largely as the measure of progress. We have seen gigantic advances in weaponry, space, gadgets, transportation, communication, organ transplants, and genetic engineering. Unfortunately, we have not made similar progress in ethical, moral, and religious values.

George Counts quotes Wernher von Braun, developer of World War II rockets, as saying: "If the world's ethical standards fail to rise with the advance of our technological revolution, we shall perish." [2] And Ellen White pictures those who, assembled before the final judgment tribunal to render an account, have failed in the value crisis. They are those who "have devoted their God-given talents of time, of means, or of intellect, to serving the gods of this world. . . . Frivolous amusements, pride of dress, indulgence of appetite, hardened the heart and benumbed the conscience. . . . Things of infinite value were lightly esteemed." [3]

Can we possibly equip our children to meet the crisis in values in our generation? Can we help them be so firm in what they believe that they will not be swayed by their environment? Let us examine a bit more closely the psychological forces with which we must contend.

A Famous Experiment

Our understanding of conformity versus values has been greatly enriched by the experimental research conducted by Stanley Milgram, of Yale University, beginning in the 1960s. Now some of the best-known studies in social psychology, the experiments originated as an effort to comprehend war atrocities in terms of the psychology of perpetrators, but they were disguised as experiments on the effect that punishment has on learning.

Volunteers were recruited by newspaper advertisement and paid well for one hour of work. Taken in pairs, the subjects drew lots to determine which one would be the "teacher" and which the "learner." The learner was strapped into a chair, and wires were attached to him. The wires led to a control panel equipped with electric switches and dials. The experimenter directed the learner in a memory learning exercise and instructed the teacher to administer electric shocks to the learner each time he gave a wrong response. The teacher was also told to administer a higher level of shock each time the learner gave a wrong answer. The control panel was labeled with voltage from 15 to 450 volts in 15-volt increments (30 switches). The switches were also designated from "slight shock" through "extreme intensity shock" and "DANGER! severe shock." The last two switches were marked XXX.

But the experiments were rigged. No real shocks were given, and the learner was an accomplice of the experimenter, trained for the role. After giving some right responses, he always acted as though he were confused, and began to miss questions badly. Shocks would be ordered by the experimenter. At 75 volts and again at 90 and 115, the learner would grunt. At 120 volts he would shout that the shocks were painful. At 135 he would groan. At 150 he would call out, "Get me out of here! I refuse to go on!" At 180 he would cry, "I can't stand the pain." At 270 he would give an agonized scream. At 300 he would refuse to provide answers. At 315 volts he would let out a violent scream and was no longer a participant. From 330 volts on he would slump in the chair in complete silence.

Nearly all the teachers found the experiment highly distressing and would turn to the experimenter for advice or to protest continuing. But the experimenter would order the teacher to administer more shocks with a series of four prods, as follows: "Please continue." "The experiment requires that you continue." "It is absolutely essential that you continue." "You have no other choice; you must go on." Only if the teacher refused at prod four would the experiment be terminated.

Psychiatrists, graduate students and faculty in the behavioral sciences, college sophomores, and middle-class adults were asked to predict the reactions. The overwhelming prediction was that virtually all subjects would refuse to obey the experimenter. It was felt that only 1 or 2 percent would proceed to the highest voltage and that these subjects would represent a pathological fringe of society. To the amazement of all, 62.5 percent of all subjects proceeded to the highest shock level.

In his report, Milgram pointed out that these citizens were not basically evil people; neither were they controlled by hostile and aggressive impulses (many protested the experiment and were highly agitated and upset). Yet they obeyed an authority figure in doing what they knew to be wrong. The study reveals the power of *conformity* as a social force. "The ordinary person who shocked the victim did so out of a sense of obligation—a conception of his duties as a subject—and not from any peculiarly aggressive tendencies." [4]

According to a thought-provoking article by Jeff Jones a few years ago in the American Psychological Association's *Monitor*, the sobering conclusion reached by Milgram was that "almost anything can be done without limitations of conscience if command to do so comes from a legitimate authority and is backed up by sufficient definitions of the situation." [5] To equip our youth to resist this psychological force must be one of the primary goals of values education.

Reflections on Watergate

The *Monitor* article reported on a symposium entitled "Obedience to Authority," featuring Milgram, two psychiatrists, and John Dean, former Presidential counsel who, no longer able to stand the strain of a life of deceit in the Watergate cover-up, exposed the plottings to the Congressional committee.

Comparing the results of Milgram's experiments with the reflections of John Dean helped to focus on the theme that well-meaning people may find themselves engaged in behavior that they would never have thought possible. Many Americans, viewing the events of Watergate, felt positively holy by comparison with "knaves" such as Nixon, Haldeman, Ehrlichman, Colson, et cetera. Yet the research seems to suggest that whatever contempt we may hold for the Watergate gang, they are like us, and we are like them. Indeed, the way these public servants handled themselves "may be largely attributable to a set of psychological dynamics to which all are more or less vulnerable."

Asked how they would personally perform under the circumstances, most people say *they* would not have administered the shocks or participated in the cover-up. "But this armchair speculation is different from the situation when the pressure is on," said Milgram. So strong are the dynamics of authority that while some subjects protested that "we shouldn't be doing this," they still went on to give the highest doses when ordered to do so by the experimenter.

Under the stress of such situations, people search for rationalizations for their behavior. Milgram pointed out: "There's a frequent modification of language so that the acts at a verbal level do not come into direct conflict with the verbal moral concepts that are a part of everyone's upbringing." In other words: "Euphemisms come to dominate the language . . . as a means of guarding the person against the full moral implications of his acts." For example, Dean reminisced about the bribes to hush the burglars: "We never talked about money; we talked about 'the bites out of the apple.' "

Dean found other ways to cope. For a time he convinced himself that in forwarding requests from the Watergate burglars for hush money, he was only acting as an agent, an intermediary, and not really participating in the cover-up. When finally he concluded that it would be better to go to jail than continue to live under such stress, his break ultimately amounted to "taking responsibility for myself." Of such is the stuff of all valuing.

The Roots of the Crisis

What are the factors today that cause many people to fail to develop value systems that can stand up to the pressures for conformity? One helpful listing includes the following:

1. The breakup of family life—the setting in which values are largely learned.

2. The mobility of modern families, resulting in a sense of rootlessness—one out of five American families moves every year.

3. The assault of television on traditional values.

4. The amoral message of many books, magazines, and other mass printing.

5. Working mothers—with both parents out of the home most of the time.

6. Widespread use of the automobile, with the opportunity to escape accountability.

7. The decline of religious influence.

8. Global wars and the threat of nuclear extinction.

9. The gap between precept and practice in the older generation—a failure of models.

10. Materialism—the emphasis placed on acquiring all sorts of possessions.

11. The multiplicity of options and choices not available to the youth of yesteryear.

12. The tendency to tell children what to do rather than

lead them to discover right values for themselves.[6]

Perhaps we could also add the modern tendency to consider all truth as relative and to believe that there are no absolute values.

Of course, pressure to surrender values in conformity to the wishes of superiors or peers has always existed. But those who have been fortunate enough to have had parents or other respected leaders who guided them in developing and committing themselves to a set of principles have found the inner strength to resist this pressure and to live up to their values.

Consider the response of the three Hebrew young men who were ordered to join the entire leadership of the nation in bowing down to the golden image on the pain of being thrown alive into a superheated furnace: "If we are thrown into the blazing furnace, the God we serve is able to save us from it, and he will rescue us from your hand, O king. But even if he does not, we want you to know, O king, that we will not serve your gods or worship the image of gold you have set up" (Dan. 3:17, 18).

Is not this the answer to the crisis in the value mart? Is not this the kind of inner moral fiber we wish to see developed in our youth? Ellen White has stated it superbly: "The greatest want of the world is the want of men—men who will not be bought or sold, men who in their inmost souls are true and honest, men who do not fear to call sin by its right name, men whose conscience is as true to duty as the needle to the pole, men who will stand for the right though the heavens fall." [7]

To produce men—and women—like this is the aim of the values education described in this book.

Notes

[1] Elliot Aronson, *The Social Animal* (San Francisco: W. H. Freeman and Co., 2d ed., 1976).

[2] George S. Counts, *Education and the Foundations of Human Freedom* (Pittsburgh: University of Pittsburgh Press, 1962), pp. 27, 28.

[3] Ellen G. White, *Patriarchs and Prophets* (Mountain View, Calif.: Pacific Press Pub. Assn., 1913), p. 558.

[4] Stanley Milgram, *Obedience to Authority: An Experimental View* (New York: Harper and Row, 1974), p. 6.

[5] Jeff Jones, "Comparing Notes on Obedience to Authority: Dean and Milgram," *APA Monitor*, January, 1978, pp. 5, 23.

[6] Louis E. Raths, Merrill Harmin, and Sidney B. Simon, *Values and Teaching* (Columbus, Ohio: Charles E. Merrill, 1966), pp. 15-26.

[7] White, *Education* (Mountain View, Calif.: Pacific Press Pub. Assn., 1903), p. 57.

CHAPTER 4

Religion: The Search for Ultimate Meaning

On an Easter Sunday morning a congregation was celebrating the resurrection of Jesus Christ in special services. As the worshipers emerged from the sanctuary into the crisp April air they found that under the windshield wiper of each car in the parking lot was a small pamphlet. Its message informed them that they were worshiping on the wrong day and should repent of their apostasy and keep the true seventh-day Sabbath.

How's that for a set of religious values? No doubt some Sabbathkeeper was congratulating himself for bearing fearless witness to the "truth." He could attribute the sense of outrage the Easter service attenders experienced to resistance of the Holy Spirit. Is this what it means to be religious?

Different types of values can be identified. In fact, every field of human endeavor has its associated value systems. *Study of Values* is an inventory based on the typology of Eduard Spranger's *Types of Men*. It aims to measure the relative strength of six basic interests or motives:

1. Theoretical Values—Seeks to discover *truth*. The chief aim is to order and systematize knowledge. Searches for identities and differences.

2. Economic Values—Emphasizes what is *useful*. Accumulates goods. Is extremely practical.

3. Aesthetic Values—Looks for *form* and *harmony*. Enjoys each event for its own sake.

4. Social Values—Centers in a *love of people*. Service and altruism are primary.

5. Political Values—Grasps for *power*. Seeks above all else personal power, influence, and renown.

6. Religious Values—Attempts to find *unity*. Seeks to comprehend cosmos. May affirm life or withdraw from it but always in regard to a higher reality.[1]

This is a book about the transmission of *religious* values. Therefore, we will not be concerned about other value viewpoints. However, it will be immediately apparent that completely separating the value areas of our lives is neither possible nor desirable. If I have strongly held religious values, they will certainly influence my economic, aesthetic, social, and political values. Of course, a nonreligious person may hold values in these various fields that have no direct connection with religion. But we will discuss these "secular" values only to the extent that they are informed by religion.

Neither will we attempt to separate moral values (based on a sense of right and wrong) from religious values, though I will allow that there are some highly moral persons who are not religious. Funk and Wagnalls *Standard College Dictionary* defines *religion* as "the beliefs, attitudes, emotions, behavior, et cetera, constituting man's relationship with the powers and principles of the universe, especially with a deity or deities." Therefore, we will focus on only those values that are determined by, or associated with, our relationship with God.

However, this still offers a very wide range, as Ellen White aptly points out: "Bible religion is not one influence among many others; its influence is to be supreme, pervading and controlling every other. It is not to be like a dash of color brushed here and there upon the canvas, but it is to pervade the whole life, as if the canvas were dipped into the color, until every thread of the fabric were dyed a deep, unfading hue." [2]

In view of this, it will be profitable to examine more closely what religion consists of before proceeding on our quest for the best means of transmitting religious values.

What Does It Mean to Be Religious?

Religion, in the Adventist context, seeks to explain the meaning of life in ultimate terms. It attempts to make sense out of existence by relating everything to an all-wise, all-powerful God who created the universe, who continually sustains it, and who has a final and benevolent purpose for His entire creation toward which He directs all history. The heart of religion is contained in the biblical statement "For in him we live and move and have our being" (Acts 17:28).

So what does it mean to be religious? The question defies a simple answer. In 1962 Charles Glock proposed five dimensions of religiosity that have become quite standard in sociological literature:

1. *Ideological:* This is the belief dimension. Every religion sets forth some beliefs to which its followers are expected to adhere.

2. *Intellectual:* This is the knowledge dimension. A religious person will be informed and knowledgeable about the basic tenets of his faith and its sacred scriptures. These first two dimensions are related. Yet belief does not necessarily follow from knowledge, nor is all belief well informed.

3. *Ritualistic:* This dimension includes various religious practices expected of adherents to a faith, such as attending church, engaging in prayer, reading the Bible, participating in the sacraments, fasting, et cetera.

4. *Experiential:* This is the extent to which a person achieves a direct knowledge of ultimate reality, senses the presence of God, or experiences religious emotion. Every religion places some value on subjective religious experience as a sign of individual religiosity.

5. *Consequential:* This dimension is somewhat different from the other four, for it describes the "secular" effects of religious belief, practice, experience, and knowledge on the individual. It measures what the adherent does or does not do as a consequence of his or her religion. It deals with the "works" side of the faith-works equation. It is more

concerned with man's relationship with his fellowman than with his relationship to God.[3]

Joseph Faulkner and Gordon DeJong constructed a questionnaire with five scales to measure Glock's dimensions. Some of the items were as follows: Ideological: beliefs about the end of the world, the nature of God, and the inspiration of the Bible (these test more universal Judeo-Christian beliefs rather than those of particular groups). Intellectual: knowledge of Creation, opinion of miracles, names of the four Gospels (some items seem to be really "beliefs"). Ritualistic: time spent on Bible reading, church attendance, marriage by religious or civil officials. Experiential: feeling of closeness to the Divine, security in the face of death, necessity of faith. Consequential: operation of nonessential business on the Sabbath, premarital sex, lying.[4]

The researchers then administered the questionnaire to 362 college students and correlated the five scales with each other. All correlations were positive and significant. In spite of possible measurement error, the findings suggest that the five dimensions do describe different aspects but that, taken together, they give a reasonable definition of what it means to be a religious person. We shall utilize all five dimensions as we proceed through these pages.

The Dangers of Religion

While this book is dedicated to the essential task of transmitting religious values, I must introduce a yellow light marked CAUTION! Religion is not necessarily good! In fact, it contains great dangers. Gordon Allport, former psychologist at Harvard and specialist in the area of religion and prejudice, demonstrates that it is a common research finding that "on the average, churchgoers are more intolerant than nonchurchgoers."[5]

Indeed, many of the greatest acts of "man's inhumanity to man" have been perpetrated in the name of religion. Allport lists some examples from the past as Augustine's appeal to the emperor to crush Pelagius, who disputed his views on damnation of unbaptized infants; John Chrysostom, the golden-tongued preacher, who persecuted the Jews, saying, "I hate the synagogue. . . . I hate the Jews"; the Crusades, with their "holy war" mentality; the horrors of the Inquisition; the Saint Bartholomew's massacre in 1572, when twenty to thirty thousand Huguenots were slaughtered; Calvin having Servetus burned at the stake for "misinterpreting the promptings of the Holy Spirit"; Queen Elizabeth I requiring Catholics to attend the Church of England; the execution of witches by the Puritan fathers; all the wars of religion; and on and on.[6]

In our day it would be easy to add the slaughter of Muslim by Hindu and vice versa in India; the killing of each other by Christians and Muslims in Lebanon, and Protestants and Catholics in Northern Ireland; and the fundamentalist Christians of America who make the building of more powerful nuclear weapons an article of their faith. The chronicle of atrocities, prejudice, and hate—all expressed under the banner of religion—would fill many books.

Nor are the dangers of religion limited to violent behavior. They are perhaps even more apparent in attitudes. Many research studies have shown that the followers of organized religion tend to be less humanitarian and have more punitive attitudes than nonreligious people. They are more likely to be intolerant toward racial and ethnic groups other than their own, tend to be more anxious, and are more often associated with mental disturbances.[7]

If I seem to be coming down rather heavily on this point, it is because I believe we must come to a basic understanding here. It is absolutely essential to take as a fundamental principle that *making a child religious is not necessarily the same thing as making him or her a good person.* Within religion are conflicting moral forces for good and evil, brotherhood and bigotry, mental peace and emotional conflict.

How can these things be? Gordon Allport proposes

three religious doctrines that may generate bigotry:

1. Doctrine of *revelation*: Truth once revealed cannot be tampered with.

2. Doctrine of *election*: One's own group is chosen and other groups are not.

3. Doctrine of *theocracy*: Rulers are divinely ordained to enforce the church's interpretation of revelation and election.

Allport then quotes 1 Corinthians 4:5 ("Judge nothing before the appointed time; wait till the Lord comes") and comments that this requires a subtle mind, "one that can embrace absolutes and at the same time judge nothing 'until the Lord comes.' " [8] A fine and delicate distinction. No wonder that building an effective value system is such a difficult undertaking.

In another work Allport explains that "the reason why churchgoers on the average are more prejudiced than nonchurchgoers is not because religion instills prejudice. It is rather that a large number of people, by virtue of their psychological makeup, require for their economy of living both prejudice and religion." [9] If they have self-doubt and insecurity, prejudice enhances their self-esteem and religion provides security. If they are guilt-ridden, prejudice provides a scapegoat and religion provides relief. If they fear failure, prejudice explains by postulating menacing outgroups, and religion holds out a reward. Both prejudice and religion satisfy the same psychological needs.

Nor is bigotry the only strange element to become mixed with religious faith. The Chicago *Tribune* of March 29, 1984 reported that a recent Gallup poll found an upsurge in America's religious interest and a similar swing toward immoral behavior. "There is no doubt that religion is growing," Gallup reported. "But we find that there is very little difference in ethical behavior between churchgoers and those who are not active religiously." He also pointed out "that the levels of lying, cheating, and stealing are remarkably similar in both groups."

Value Systems in Religion

A crucial question then is Do those who are religious have a distinctive system of moral values that sets them apart from the less religious and the nonreligious? Rokeach reports on such a study,[10] which used 1,400 adults in a National Opinion Research Center survey and 300 Michigan State University students. The subjects were asked to rank his eighteen terminal values (preferred end-states of existence) and his eighteen instrumental values (preferred modes of behavior) in order of perceived importance as guiding principles in their daily lives. To separate the religious from the nonreligious, three criteria were used:

1. Membership in a denomination, or no affiliation.
2. Frequency of church attendance.
3. The question, How important is religion to you in your everyday life? (This is referred to by behavioral scientists as *saliency*.)

For the terminal values, weekly church attenders ranked "salvation" third, while nonattenders ranked it eighteenth. Churchgoers were significantly lower on "a comfortable life," "an exciting life," "freedom," and "pleasure." For the instrumental values, churchgoers were significantly higher on "forgiving," "helpful," and "obedient," while nongoers were higher on "imaginative," "independent," and "logical."

Those who found religion most salient ranked "salvation" higher on the terminal values than did the others. For the instrumental values, those high on saliency ranked moral values (clean, forgiving, helpful, obedient, polite, honest, loving, and self-controlled) high in comparison with subjects low on saliency. The latter tended to rate competence values (capable, imaginative, intellectual, logical, ambitious, broad-minded, and independent) high. "When magnitude of value difference was considered . . . , two values, salvation and forgiving, were found to be the most distinctively Christian values."

So religion does make a difference in a person's values.

But wait! Before we cheer, let us inquire as to what kind of a difference. Specifically, to what extent are the moral values espoused by the religious related to a compassionate social outlook? In other words, are religious people kinder and more loving—better neighbors?

Rokeach went on to compare the rankings on "salvation" and "forgiving" (religious values) with responses to a number of questions on social compassion. What did he find? Those who place a high value on "salvation" are conservative, eager to maintain the status quo, and generally more indifferent and unsympathetic with the plight of the black and the poor. They were more likely to react to the Martin Luther King, Jr., assassination (a recent event) with "he brought it on himself" than with sadness, anger, or shame. When presented with thirteen civil rights issues (fair employment, racial equality, et cetera), they were significantly lower on *every one of them* than those who ranked salvation low.

In seven out of eleven attitudes toward the poor, those ranking salvation high were significantly more negative than those who ranked it lower. They were more opposed to the church's involvement in social issues. The same pattern held for church attendance. Frequent churchgoers were found to be somewhat less compassionate than less frequent goers. "One may well wonder, after seeing these data," Rokeach concludes, "whether Marx was right after all when he suggested that religion is the opiate of the people."

Even though this study has received some criticism on methodological grounds, its findings are pretty much in line with other research. Do we even *want* to transmit religious values? Will we be creating only self-satisfied bigots? But surely all religion can't be like that! As a matter of fact, it isn't. And if we are to be faithful to our mission of developing values in the younger generation, we had better know the difference. This will be the object of our search in the next chapter.

Notes

[1] Gordon W. Allport, Philip E. Vernon, and Gardner Lindzey, *Manual: Study of Values* (Boston: Houghton Mifflin Company, 1970), pp. 3-5.

[2] Ellen G. White, *The Desire of Ages* (Mountain View, Calif.: Pacific Press Pub. Assn., 1940), p. 312.

[3] Charles Y. Glock, "On the Study of Religious Commitment," *Religious Education Research Supplement* 57 (July-August, 1962): 98-110.

[4] Joseph E. Faulkner and Gordon F. DeJong, "Religiosity in 5-D: An Empirical Analysis," *Social Forces* 45 (December, 1966): pp. 246-254.

[5] Gordon W. Allport, *Personality and Social Encounter* (Boston: Beacon Press, 1960), p. 257.

[6] *Ibid.*, pp. 259-261.

[7] See Rokeach, *Beliefs, Attitudes, and Values*, pp. 189-196.

[8] Allport, *op. cit.*, pp. 258, 259.

[9] ———, "The Religious Context of Prejudice," *Journal for the Scientific Study of Religion* 5 (Fall, 1966): 451.

[10] Milton Rokeach, "The H. Paul Douglass Lectures for 1969," *Review of Religious Research* 11 (Fall, 1969): 3-39.

CHAPTER 5

Two Types of Religion

Religious people care mainly about their own personal salvation and receiving "the blessings of the Lord" in this life but are largely unconcerned about the plight of others. They are smug in their status as an in-group and tend to look down on "sinners," who are beneath them. They shore up their own insecurities by a close-minded grasping of inflexible dogma. At least, that's what the voluminous research on religion and prejudice seems to indicate, as I reported in the previous chapter.

But that just can't be true! What about Christians such as Mother Teresa, Albert Schweitzer, and my own saintly grandmother, who was constantly finding practical ways to demonstrate the love of Christ to those less fortunate? No matter what the research says, many of us have been blessed by the presence of a loving God through the lives of His followers.

Only one possible resolution to this dilemma presents itself. Religion comes in two types—one self-centered and bigoted and the other self-sacrificing and altruistic. Scientific research has given religion a bad press by largely measuring the former type, which is, unfortunately, the far more common of the two.

Jesus often contrasted these two types. He told a story of a man badly beaten and left for dead by robbers (Luke 10:25-37). A priest and a Levite (both religious leaders of the nation) came along. But they passed him by, unwilling to involve themselves. Then the good Samaritan came. He "took pity on him," "bandaged his wounds," "took him to an inn and took care of him." This illustrates what keeping God's law is all about, according to Jesus.

Again, Jesus told about two men who went to the temple to pray (chap. 18:9-14). The Pharisee (a religious teacher) "prayed about himself; 'God, I thank you that I am not like all other men.' " But the tax collector bowed down and cried, "God, have mercy on me, a sinner." Jesus made it clear that the tax collector and not the Pharisee went home justified.

In an awesome passage (Matt. 25:31-46) Jesus describes the final judgment as separating people on the basis of what they had done in His name for the hungry, the thirsty, the outcast, the ill-clothed, the sick, and the prisoner. Ellen White's comment is penetrating: "He represented its [the great judgment day] decision as turning upon one point. When the nations are gathered before Him, there will be but two classes, and their eternal destiny will be determined by what they have done or have neglected to do for Him in the person of the poor and the suffering." [1]

So the concept of two types of religion is not a new one. Jesus directed His most scathing rebukes against religious people (Matthew 23). It will be interesting to note that contemporary students of religion have discovered the same distinction.

Dichotomies of Religion

Early in his studies, Allport, following the lead of Lenski, defined two types of religious experience: communal and associational.[2] Communal people affiliate with a church because it is in fashion to do so. The church provides status and serves as gossip center, meeting place for the lonely, and source of entertainment. Religion has its rewards but has little effect on the way these people conduct their daily affairs. Associational people, on the other hand, seek involvement primarily for purposes of religious fellowship.

Russell Allen and Bernard Spilka[3] reviewed the literature and discovered several bipolar religious orientations that have been proposed. In each set the first pole represents the more prejudiced orientation:

1. Authoritarian versus humanistic.
2. Fundamentalism versus humanitarianism.
3. Unstable conviction versus stable conviction.
4. Lower value system versus higher value system.
5. Devotional approach versus conventional approach.
6. Emphasis on religious rites and practices versus personal relationship to the Deity.
7. Conventional, externalized, neutralized orientation versus personal and internalized orientation.
8. Extrinsic versus intrinsic orientation.

All of this is consistent with 2 Timothy 3:1-5, which informs us, "There will be terrible times in the last days." The passage goes on to catalog a list of inhumanities that *are committed by religious people,* for the perpetrators are described as "having a form of godliness but denying its power."

Extrinsic and Intrinsic Religion

Since a great deal of research has investigated the extrinsic-intrinsic dimension, let us look more closely at this concept, which is really more of a continuum than a dichotomy. Allport, who has popularized this model, explains: "*Extrinsic* religion is a self-serving, utilitarian, self-protective form of religious outlook, which provides the believer with comfort and salvation at the expense of out-groups. *Intrinsic* religion marks the life that has interiorized the total creed of his faith without reservation, including the commandment to love one's neighbor. A person of this sort is more intent on serving his religion than on making it serve him. In many lives both strands are found; the result is inner conflict, with prejudice and tolerance competing for the upper hand." [4]

Some of the varieties of extrinsic religious orientation are: (1) those involved in church activities but not in the spiritual dimensions, (2) those who are casual and peripheral churchgoers but not highly committed, and (3) those on the extreme right or the extreme left. All point to a type of religion "strictly utilitarian; useful for the self in granting safety, social standing, solace, and endorsement for one's chosen way of life." [5]

In contrast, intrinsic religion "regards faith as a supreme value in its own right. It is oriented toward a unification of being, takes seriously the commandment of brotherhood, and strives to transcend all self-centered needs. Dogma is tempered with humility." [6]

Although religion has been a source of strength in the lives of many of us, it has sometimes been misused to promote an unhealthy dependency where one person or group controls the behavior and makes the decisions for another. Rollo May holds that religion could be a source of strength or a source of weakness, depending upon how it is used. Is it a flight from reality, a release from responsibility, a shoring up of anxieties, a crutch for insecurities, a fostering of dependency? Or is it a courageous endeavor to understand reality better, a reasoning from principle to action, a promotion of personal growth and love toward each other?[7]

May explains that Jesus, in the Sermon on the Mount, shifted the ethical emphasis from external rules to *inward* motives. To be "pure in heart" means that the external actions are at one with the inner motives. He reminds us that Kierkegaard titled one of his booklets: "Purity of Heart Is to Will One Thing." [8]

Without using the labels, Ellen White highlights the extrinsic-intrinsic contrast in her comments on the stony-ground hearers in the parable of the sower: "Many receive the gospel as a way of escape from suffering, rather than as a deliverance from sin. They rejoice for a season, for they think that religion will free them from difficulty and trial. While life moves smoothly with them, they may appear to be consistent Christians. But they faint beneath the fiery test of temptation. They cannot bear reproach for Christ's sake. When the word of God points out some cherished sin, or requires self-denial or sacrifice, they are offended." [9]

How Do We Get That Way?

Allport[10] proposes that the development of an extrinsic orientation may begin with a child who is insecure and feels inferior. He/she is taught that all other religions are inferior to the one held by the parents. The child decides that God is partial and one can secure His special favor to "get on top." "In such a life religion is not the cause of . . . prejudice" or vice versa. "Both strategies are protective; both confer security, a sense of status and of encapsulation." It is easy for people to assume that God meant to arrange the human family in hierarchical order with themselves on top. Scripture may be cited to prove the point. The result?

"Religion is not the master motive in the life. It plays an instrumental role only. It serves and rationalizes assorted forms of self-interest. . . . The full creed and full teaching of religion are not adopted. The person does not serve his religion; it is subordinated to serve him. The master-motive is always self-interest. In such a life-economy, religion has extrinsic value only." [11]

And what of intrinsic religion? The youngster has the benefit of basic trust and security within the home and doesn't need to look at other people as a threat to personal well-being. By adolescence he/she achieves *reciprocity*, the ability to perceive that others have convictions and preferences that are—from their point of view—as reasonable as one's own. Advancing into maturity, this youth does not necessarily lose the childhood religious faith or even belief in specific revelation and election, "but dogma is tempered with humility; in keeping with biblical injunction, he withholds judgment until the day of the harvest. A religious sentiment of this sort floods the whole life with motivation and meaning. It is no longer limited to single segments of self-interest. And only in such a widened religious sentiment does the teaching of brotherhood take firm root." [12]

Religion as Relationships

What does all this mean to us? Just this. Before trying to transmit religious values, we need to think carefully of what kind of person we wish to produce. Do we want children to grow up into adults who hold to a rigid religious code but who selfishly use its benefits to promote their own temporal or eternal welfare without regard for those "poor sinners" who are beneath them? Or do we want people whose lives are an outpouring of love for God and their fellow humans? In short, do we wish to encourage extrinsic or intrinsic religion?

If the latter, then we will need to see and to teach religion as a matter of relationships rather than as a list of commands and prohibitions. First and central to all else is a relationship with God as a loving Father and friend. Jesus went to the very core of religion when He stated, "Love the Lord your God with all your heart and with all your soul and with all your mind. This is the first and greatest commandment" (Matt. 22:37, 38).

Following from this, religion works in our own interior relationships, eliminating anxiety and stress and bringing harmony and peace of mind. Jesus spoke of this when He said, "Peace I leave with you; my peace I give you. . . . Do not let your hearts be troubled and do not be afraid" (John 14:27).

Out of this twofold relationship with God and with ourselves comes a new relationship with our fellow humans. The second greatest commandment is to "love your neighbor as yourself" (Matt. 22:39).

Let us admit that this has not always been our approach to religious values education. *Adventist Review* columnist Miriam Wood received a request to "please give me a firm definition of what it means to be worldly. I want you to prepare a list of do's and don'ts in detail." Have any of us ever suffered from that kind of mentality? Wood wisely replied, in part: "It is not in my nature to approach God and religion this way. I do not see the great plan of salvation as a legalistic formula, but rather as a manifestation of divine love that causes us to honor God in all that we do. . . . The genius of Bible religion is the personal relationship between each soul and God." [13]

When Jesus refused to apply the law in such a way as to condemn the woman caught in the act of adultery to be stoned (John 8:1-11), He showed us that codes must minister to the needs of human beings created in the image of God and not be lovelessly enforced. When accused by religious leaders of breaking the Sabbath to satisfy the hunger of the disciples, He replied, "The Sabbath was made for man, not man for the Sabbath" (Mark 2:27). Jesus constantly taught and modeled religion as relationships.

In an earlier work I reported on a study of four hundred adolescents with religious backgrounds. A measure of their concepts of religion ranging from legalism to a personal relationship with a loving God was found to be significantly correlated with a measure of their alienation from religion and the church. This means that youth "who see religion as a system of rules and regulations are more likely to be alienated from it than those who understand religion to consist of a personal relationship with God." [14]

The "two types of religion" model will be a central pillar in our thinking as we journey through this book.

PASSING ON THE TORCH

Notes

[1] White, *The Desire of Ages,* p. 637.

[2] Allport, "The Religious Context of Prejudice," *Journal for the Scientific Study of Religion* 5, p. 452.

[3] Russell O. Allen and Bernard Spilka, "Committed and Consensual Religion: A Specification of Religion-Prejudice Relationships," *Journal for the Scientific Study of Religion* 6 (Fall, 1967): 191-206.

[4] Allport, *Personality and Social Encounter,* p. 257.

[5] Allport, "The Religious Context of Prejudice," *op. cit.,* p. 455.

[6] *Ibid.*

[7] Rollo May, *Man's Search for Himself* (New York: W.W. Norton, 1953), pp. 205, 206.

[8] *Ibid.,* p. 221.

[9] Ellen G. White, *Christ's Object Lessons* (Washington, D.C.: Review and Herald Pub. Assn., 1941), p. 47.

[10] Allport, *Personality and Social Encounter,* p. 263, 264.

[11] *Ibid.*

[12] *Ibid.,* p. 265.

[13] *Adventist Review,* May 12, 1983, p. 10.

[14] Roger L. Dudley, *Why Teenagers Reject Religion and What to Do About It* (Washington, D.C.: Review and Herald Pub. Assn., 1978), pp. 71, 72.

CHAPTER 6

Choosing the Best Values

Years ago I heard theology professor Paul Heubach, relate a fascinating story. A young man roaming the fields and woods stumbled onto the mouth of a hidden cave. His curiosity aroused, he made his way through a winding passage and found himself in a dimly lighted cavern. As his eyes became accustomed to the semidarkness he realized that he was in a treasure house. Everywhere were gold and silver vessels, coins of precious metal, and sparkling jewelry.

As he began to gather what he deemed to be some of the more valuable pieces he heard a voice. Surprised, he turned to see an old man sitting to one side.

"Take all you want, son," the voice said gently. "Only be sure that you choose the best."

The youth was somewhat confused, for he thought that was what he had been doing. Nevertheless, he emptied his pockets and began the selection process anew.

But again the gentle reminder, "Take all you want, son. Only be sure that you choose the best."

Laying aside what he had gathered, the young man searched carefully until he felt that he had certainly chosen the most valuable of the treasures. He filled his pockets and loaded a sack with all that he could possibly carry. Then he carefully inched his way out of the cave and started for home as rapidly as possible. After some distance he tired and sat down to rest. He decided to examine his new possessions more closely. He was shocked to discover that his pockets and sack contained only dry leaves!

Only a legend—perhaps a parable. It no doubt contains a number of possible lessons. For our purposes one interpretation will be sufficient. We may think we are choosing the best values in life—even religious values—only to discover later that our choice has netted us nothing but "dry leaves."

Choice Is Vital

Some methods of value education focus on helping young people to clarify and articulate the values they really believe in but that may be vague or unstructured in their minds. While this is a worthwhile task and one that I shall deal with later in this book, it is not enough. It is based on the assumption that all carefully considered values are appropriate and that some values should not be considered better than others a priori. But a person might go through the valuing process and actually select discrimination, abuse, or exploitation as most worthwhile values. Even in religion, as we have seen in the previous chapter, some values are far superior to others.

Educators divide values into two classes: *Group-specific* values are widely shared within one group or society but have little meaning to those not in that group. A conservative church such as the Seventh-day Adventist will have many; for example: proper activities for Sabbath, dietary regulations, use of jewelry, standards of recreation and entertainment, et cetera. On the other hand, *abstract universal* values describe those that would be affirmed (but not necessarily practiced) by nearly all thoughtful people. They include values such as equality, justice, brotherhood, self-respect, respect for others, developing responsible behavior, tolerance for varying views.[1]

If we are to produce adults who determine their behavior by a set of carefully considered principles and whose religion promotes a deeper relationship between God and man and between man and man—people with intrinsic religion—we must give priority to the abstract universal values in our program of moral education.

This is not to say that group-specific values are not important. Indeed, they are the qualities that give uniqueness to any community. Wash them out and the group may as well blend into the larger society. They are its raison d'être as a separate entity. But if we concentrate on specifics first in our transmission of values, we may well produce youth who have codes of behavior but no integrated system of principles; who are legalistic but not loving; who have some worthwhile rules but no overarching framework in which to locate them. We need to place primary emphasis on the larger picture of relationships and then fit the specific values into this total life pattern, to begin with the general and move to the particular.

Perhaps you may be thinking that the abstract universal values are not really religious. Some even may be labeling them "humanistic," a term that has come, in the minds of many conservative religionists, to represent all that is wrong in the world. But values are not in themselves religious or nonreligious. The difference between religion and secular humanism is not in the content of the values but in the framework from which life is approached and in the reasons for behaviors. While the value of "equality," for example, may be held without regard to religion, it may also be strongly influenced by my relationship with God and what He tells me about my relationship with my fellow humans. The same is true, of course, for group-specific values. My dietary practices may be based in religious experience or formed entirely without regard for ultimate concerns.

So choosing the best religious values is vital. The Bible illustrates this in the story of Solomon's request (1 Kings 3:5-14). God had given him an incredible blank check: "Ask for whatever you want me to give you." Solomon's choice? "Give your servant a discerning heart to govern your people and to distinquish between right and wrong." Notice the universal rather than the specific nature of the choice. "The Lord was pleased that Solomon had asked for this." As a result, God not only granted Solomon's request but promised him a number of specific blessings that he would be able to utilize effectively as long as he continued to have his cosmic values straight.

Ellen White also emphasizes correct choice in religious values when she writes that we should study God's purpose in the history of nations in order "that we may estimate at their true value things seen and things unseen; that we may learn what is the true aim of life; that, viewing the things of time in the light of eternity, we may put them to their truest and noblest use." [2]

Values in Relationship to God

We have already discussed the concept of teaching religion as a set of relationships rather than as a system of beliefs or a code of behaviors. Fundamental to the whole network of relationships is the relationship with God. "Love the Lord your God with all your heart and with all your soul and with all your mind. This is the first and greatest commandment" (Matt. 22:37, 38). The highest values concern making God the center of our lives and recognizing our complete dependence on Him. We learn to turn to Him joyously, as the flower turns to the sun. Only in this context do specific religious behaviors have any meaning.

What, then, is the most serious sin? Is it murder, unchastity, theatregoing, anger, greed, or drunkenness? George Knight replies: "The biblical answer is a resounding no! It is pride. Pride is linked to self-centeredness, self-sufficiency, and an unhealthy self-love—a frame of mind which induces us to trust in our own goodness, strength, and wisdom rather than to rely upon the Creator-God. . . . It is an attitude that places the universal center of meaning on the individual self rather than upon God. In pride and self-sufficiency we find the essence of sin." [3]

Indeed, sin originated in the universe when Lucifer said, "I will make myself like the Most High" (Isa. 14:14). Sin began on this planet when Eve believed the serpent, which told her, "You will be like God, knowing good and evil" (Gen. 3:5). It can be argued that the basic definition of sin is a breaking of relationships with the Creator and Sustainer—being out of harmony with Him. "Everything that does not come from faith is sin" (Rom. 14:23).

What is the purpose of life? "Fear God and give him glory" (Rev. 14:7). Again, to "fear God and keep his commandments" is described as "the whole duty of man" (Eccl. 12:13). The requirements of religion are crisply summed up as "to act justly and to love mercy and to walk humbly with your God" (Micah 6:8).

In her approach to religious valuing, Ellen White gives the more cosmic view as opposed to narrow specifics:

"Make an honest reckoning. Put into one scale Jesus, which means eternal treasure, life, truth, heaven, and the joy of Christ in souls redeemed; put into the other every attraction the world can offer. Into one scale put the loss of your own soul, and the souls of those whom you might have been instrumental in saving; into the other, for yourself and for them, a life that measures with the life of God. Weigh for time and for eternity." [4]

This concept of religion is a positive one. Many Christians struggle with a constant sense of guilt and defeat because they see no hope of measuring up to the impossible code of behavior demanded of them. It is not God's will, however, that His children shall live in despair. "Do not be afraid, little flock, for your Father has been pleased to give you the kingdom" (Luke 12:32). When we allow God to be at the center of our lives, we ally ourselves with the most powerful force in the universe—one that never knows failure. The entire religious experience is transformed. Ellen White expresses it this way:

"God has given the youth a ladder to climb, a ladder that reaches from earth to heaven. Above this ladder is God, and on every round fall the bright beams of His glory. He is watching those who are climbing, ready, when the grasp relaxes and the steps falter, to send help. Yes, tell it in words full of cheer, that no one who perseveringly climbs the ladder will fail of gaining an entrance into the heavenly city." [5]

It is this larger picture of the God-centered life that must form the foundation of our efforts toward value transmission if we would develop a generation to whom religion is more than a cloak or a crutch.

Values in Relationships to People

If the first cosmic area of values is found in our relationship with God, the second flows naturally from it—our relationships with other people. "The second [greatest commandment] is . . . 'Love your neighbor as yourself' " (Matt. 22:39). These values affirm the worth and dignity of *people*. People matter. They should be treated with consideration, respect, and Christlike love, no matter how undeserving they may seem to be. In each fellow human we are to discern the image of God. Remember that the admonition of Jesus to "be perfect" (chap. 5:48) was given in the context of loving the unlovely.

Knight notes that "since the root of evil is found in self-centeredness, it follows that the antithesis of this would be that good is rooted in other-centeredness." [6] The highest values concern relating with God (dependence) and relating with fellow humans (service).

Recently I heard Dr. Jasmine Jacob relate an experience she had in India some years back. Having gone there to conduct workshops for teachers, she traveled extensively and, for the first time, came to understand something of that great nation's poverty and need. At one appointment she found a 10-year-old boy sweeping floors in the middle of the morning. She asked him why he was not in school. Tears flowed down his face as he answered that his parents were both dead, and he was trying to earn enough for a little food. He had slept in the school doorway the previous night, hoping someone would give him some menial task.

Stirred to the depths of compassion, Jacob came home to found and lead REACH International. Today thousands of children in nine Third World countries receive food, lodging, and a Christian education because of her tireless dedication. Could any religious value system be more worthy of transmission? Ellen White comments: "We might have been in the place of the poor souls who are in error. According to the truth that we have received above others, we are debtors to impart the same to them." [7]

Or consider the values pervading this statement attributed to General William Booth, founder of the Salvation Army, at 83 years of age—just three months before his death:

"While women weep as they do now, I'll fight; while little children go hungry as they do now, I'll fight; while men go to prison, in and out, in and out, I'll fight; while there yet remains one dark soul without the light of God, I'll fight—I'll fight to the very end!"

This value calls for us not to discriminate or show partiality on the basis of any external characteristic. It calls for us to leave the judging of motives to God and simply be agents to reveal His love. Ellen White explains:

"All were created in His image, and even the most degraded are to be treated with respect and tenderness. God will hold us accountable for even a word spoken in contempt of one soul for whom Christ laid down His life." [8]

The purpose of religious value education is to produce adults with this larger sense of compassion. If we make instead the conformity to specific codes of behavior our major focus, we may well find religiously narrow people at the other end of the process.

Writing to teachers, Russell Argent explains: "A Christian teacher must also be unafraid to show anger to his students in the presence of cruelty, racial prejudice, and immorality. To live in moral neutrality would be to betray his faith. Yet he should be careful about the source of his outrage. Ever-changing social mores, on the periphery of life, are not always important to spiritual growth. Students must not think that the most exciting message of the church is a crusade against banal films, noisy music, and sloppy dress.

"Teachers instead should convey to their students the unchanging principles of honesty, decency, love, and compassion. Such teachers can never fail, for their lives will touch the lives of others in hidden ways. Worldiness is not identified by a list of 'do's' or 'don'ts.' Instead, it is putting oneself at the center of things and shutting God out. The student who meets the compassionate love of the risen Christ in an Adventist academy and college will successfully survive the questions and temptations he will meet in a secular society." [9]

I believe that this says it well, though I do not deny the importance of specific values once a framework of cosmic values has been constructed into which they can be fitted. A popular magazine quoted singer Pearl Bailey as being tired of hearing parents say, "I'm going to give my children what I didn't have." Pearl said she was going to give her children what she *did* have, such things as good manners and how to treat people with compassion. Thus in a things-obsessed world, she gave an affirmation of the superiority of human, moral values.

This can be summed up by the wisdom of the eighteenth-century philosopher Immanuel Kant, who wrote: "So act to treat humanity, whether in thine own person or in that of any other, in every case as an end withal, never as means only." Appropriate religious values lead those who hold them to *serve* people rather than to *use* them.

Notes

[1] Margaret Edwards Arcus. "Value Reasoning: An Approach to Values Education," *Family Relations* 29 (April, 1980): 163-171.

[2] White, *Education,* p. 184.

[3] Knight, *Philosophy and Education,* p. 164.

[4] White, *Christ's Object Lessons,* p. 374.

[5] ———, *Messages to Young People* (Nashville: Southern Pub. Assn., 1923), p. 95.

[6] Knight, *op. cit.,* p. 164.

[7] Ellen G. White, *Evangelism* (Washington, D.C.: Review and Herald Pub. Assn., 1946), p. 218.

[8] ———, *Thoughts From the Mount of Blessing* (Mountain View, Calif.: Pacific Press Pub. Assn., 1956), p. 57.

[9] Russell H. Argent, "Compassion: The Heartbeat of Christian Education," *The Journal of Adventist Education* 45 (April-May, 1983): 47.

CHAPTER 7

Cut Flowers or Living Plants

One of the most heart-tugging books I have ever read is Viktor Frankl's *From Death Camp to Existentialism*. Frankl lucidly details his experiences as a prisoner in several German World War II concentration camps. In this stressful environment the veneer of human dignity and decency is stripped away. Survival becomes the only rule. In its pursuit men shamelessly exploit their fellow humans or, at best, have no concern for their plight. The most shocking human suffering has no power to move those who have become totally self-centered.

Yet even in this nadir of common humanity, an occasional bright light illuminates the darkness. Frankl recalls:

"We who lived in concentration camps can remember the men who walked through the huts comforting others, giving away their last piece of bread. They may have been few in number, but they offer sufficient proof that everything can be taken from a man but one thing: the last of the human freedoms—to choose one's attitude in any given set of circumstances, to choose one's own way. It is this spiritual freedom—which cannot be taken away—that makes life meaningful and purposeful." [1]

Would you not like to see young people with a value so integrated into their very being that, though everything else could be taken from them, it could not? It is this value that we must consider in the present chapter.

In the last chapter we noted that some religious values are more fundamental, more cosmic, more overarching than others and that these values should receive priority in moral education. We identified two major categories based on relationships to God and relationships to fellow humans. But providing a connecting link between these two areas are relationships with the inner self. While we cannot explore individually each value in this category, one is so foundational to the whole process of value formation that a failure to understand it renders the remainder of this book meaningless. It will be well worth a few pages of our consideration.

We might call it "freedom." However, I am referring to bondage not of the human body but of the mind. We might call it "independence" in the best sense of the word. Or perhaps it is "free will" in its theological meaning, or "choice of destiny." At any rate, it is thinking critically for oneself. It is that risk that God took when He placed the forbidden tree in the Garden of Eden so that Adam and Eve could freely decide how they wished to relate to His kingship. It is God saying, "Come now, let us reason together" (Isa. 1:18). It is the closing appeal of Scripture: "Whosoever will, let him take the water of life freely" (Rev. 22:17, KJV).

Obedience or Freedom

Those of us who are parents or teachers or are otherwise involved with young people are rightly concerned with value education. We know that it is not enough that our youth learn facts and skills. Knowing the truth about Christian doctrines and behaviors is only the first step. How they feel about these truths and what they decide to do about them is what really counts.

Therefore we fear that our children and adolescents may not choose correct attitudes and behaviors and will lose their way. In our anxiety and our compulsion to do something, we often fool ourselves into believing that we can pass important values directly to the youth. Often our method has been to teach and preach what we believe to be right and then expect conformity. If this conformity is slow in coming, we use various disciplinary measures to attempt to secure it.

But values and principled behavior should not be identified with obedience. I have a little white poodle who is very obedient. She will sit in our yard and gaze at other dogs and at people. She will wag her tail in anticipation of a friendly encounter, but she will not leave the yard, because I have told her not to. This is very commendable, and I praise her lavishly. In no way, however, do I infer from this that she is a creature with a highly developed sense of ethical principles. So in young people. The mere fact that a child can mouth back the lesson I have taught him or comply to a standard that I have set up for him does not mean that he is developing a set of values.

Now, I do not mean to suggest that I favor *disobedience* or that small children should not be taught to obey. Learning obedience is an important part of the growing-up process for a number of reasons. But obedience must not be confused with internalized values. As the child grows into the teenager, the need increases for him (or her) to think through ethical problems and make choices that are truly his own. He must question the values of his elders and struggle with the issues involved until he develops a value system that he can personally believe in and to which he is willing to commit himself.

While freedom and obedience are not necessarily opposed to each other, the value of freedom of thinking for oneself must sometimes lead to disobedience. Thus it did when the apostles, ordered by the religious authorities to cease preaching Jesus, replied, "We must obey God rather than men" (Acts 5:29)! Thus it was that Christians in mid-nineteenth-century America broke the fugitive slave laws as they aided black escapees along the Underground Railroad. For this reason men and women languish in prisons for preaching their faith in certain atheistic countries of the world today. And religious leaders broke unjust laws in the civil rights protests of the 1960s. True values and ethical behavior are related more to freedom and choice than they are to obedience.

Freedom Is Positive

Of course, in these cases the freedom was really obedience to a higher authority. Principled freedom is never just contrariness. But one must have such an internal sense of what is right that he or she is willing to disobey the immediate power in quest of the larger good. Rollo May shows that freedom is not rebellion—a negative concept— or not planlessness or laissez-faire. Rather, "freedom is man's capacity to take a hand in his own development. It is our capacity to mold ourselves. . . . By our power to be conscious of ourselves, we can call to mind how we acted yesterday or last month, and by learning from these actions we can influence, even if ever so little, how we act today." [2]

Further, "Freedom is involved when we accept the realities not by blind necessity but by choice." [3] We are reminded that Kierkegaard's expression "choosing one's self" means "to affirm one's responsibility for one's self and one's existence." May quotes Goethe: "He only earns his freedom and existence who daily conquers them anew." [4]

In the autumn of 1982 the religion editor of the New York *Times* visited the campus of Andrews University and interviewed faculty and students about the beliefs of the Seventh-day Adventist Church. In the October 13 issue of the *Student Movement* the student editor wrote in part:

"I haven't always been the most daring or explosive in my theology. Very often I was caught in what I was taught to believe. With him sitting in the office I began to explore some of my personal limits as an independently thinking Christian. I decided I was a Christian, but what I hadn't decided was if I was willing to risk the traditional for the personal attitude of searching for the whys of my belief. Had I ever risked anything at all? . . .

"When he left, I stopped to think. It was then I realized the importance of using our decision-making faculties to their maximum capacity. Sometimes we become so mechanical in nature, we expect to be told what we should believe. As children it was necessary to be guided, even tugged, in the proper direction. This usually continues into adolescence, but somewhere along the line the mindless following should stop. . . .

"Just because a student has become an independent thinker, looking for answers further than his teachers or papers does not necessarily tag him as a revolutionary. He is but attempting to salvage what can be his most precious possession—his mind."

Here we have the rare opportunity actually to observe this young woman in the process of value formation. While we cannot say with certainty exactly where this questioning process may lead, we can be sure of one thing. Without engaging in this struggle, she will never possess the kind of principles that cannot be taken away from her whatever else she might lose.

Ellen White explains: "The discipline of a human being who has reached the years of intelligence should differ from the training of a dumb animal [like my poodle]. . . . It is not God's purpose that any mind should be thus dominated. Those who weaken or destroy individuality assume a responsibility that can result only in evil. While under authority, the children may appear like well-drilled soldiers; but when the control ceases, the character will be found to lack strength and steadfastness." [5]

All this illustrates what I have previously said about the two types of religion. If religion only fosters a dependency upon some parental or ecclesiastical authority, if it causes you to put your mind in neutral, if it calls for blind, unreasoning belief, then it may well deserve the charge of its critics that it is the "enemy of morality." A religion worth transmitting is a careful consideration of the evidence, a studied shift from external human authority to the internal authority of the enlightened conscience.

Valuing for Myself

No matter how good or right values may be in themselves, the success of value education lies in helping the youth to have power to do the valuing. To be prepared for responsible adulthood, adolescents must develop the inner capacity to experience values (including beliefs, attitudes, and behaviors) as real and worthwhile *for themselves*. Ellen White explains: "Every human being, created in the image of God, is endowed with a power akin to that of the Creator—individuality, power to think and to do. . . . It is the work of true education to develop this power, to train the youth to be thinkers, and not mere reflectors of other men's thought." [6]

The need is to produce adults who are "strong to think and to act," who are "masters and not slaves of circumstances," and who "possess breadth of mind, clearness of thought, and the courage of their convictions." [7] In another work she counsels parents to "teach your children to reason from cause to effect." [8] This is as true in moral development as it is in other phases of education.

Writes May, "Unless the individual himself can affirm the value, unless his own inner motives, his own ethical awareness, are made the starting place, no discussion of values will make much real difference." [9] The youth must come to the place where he or she can say with conviction: "To the best of my lights at the moment this is what I choose to do, even though I may know more and choose differently tomorrow." [10]

This calls for the kind of inner integrity and harmony that can come only from carefully considered and thoughtfully chosen values. "An ethical man does not act on the conscious level as though he loves someone when on unconscious levels he hates him. . . . One has endeavored to act as nearly as possible from the 'center' of himself." [11]

So youth will choose values. The questions are How can we encourage them in the process of valuing? and How can we guide them in better, more principled ways of establishing values? The answer lies not in preaching our values to them. Studies to be considered have shown that direct instruction has little lasting effect on character development. Nor does it lie in trying to force our values upon them. With teenagers this method almost assures that they will become hostile toward these values and reject them.

Rather, we must not only permit but encourage teenagers to question our value statements. This is not easy to do. We are naturally drawn to the conforming, obedient youth who affirms our position; we feel uncomfortable in the presence of the critical one who "makes waves." If we are honest, we will admit that we have usually reinforced agreement rather than questioning. But we *must* press adolescents to raise the questions, identify the issues, and think through to the solutions, or they will reach adulthood with a set of "values" that can easily collapse and disappear in a crisis because they have never been personally committed to them.

May makes a helpful distinction when he explains that the battle is not between individual freedom and tradition but in how tradition is to be used.[12] The authoritarian asks, What does the tradition require of me? The free person inquires, What does the tradition have to teach me about human life, in my particular time and with my problems?

To allow freedom is risky. It will take courage on the part of the keeper of the values as well as courage from the youth who must accept the awful responsibility of making life's great decisions. May holds that it requires greater courage to preserve inner freedom than to stand defiantly for outer freedom.[13] The opposite of courage is not cowardice but conformity in an automaton-like manner.[14]

According to Ellen White this is indeed a moral issue: "The education that consists in the training of the memory, tending to discourage independent thought, has a *moral bearing* which is too little appreciated. As the student sacrifices the power to reason and judge for himself, he becomes incapable of discriminating between truth and error, and falls an easy prey to deception. He is easily led to follow tradition and custom."[15]

I will never forget my sixth-grade teacher. Most of that year is only a blur (it was a long time ago), but she had a favorite expression that remains clear in my mind after all these years. When she would ask a question (and each of her questions had only one right answer), and the student (sometimes Roger) would respond with "Well, I think . . . ," she would usually snap, "And who gave you permission to think?" Even today the message is clear: "Your job is to learn material and give it back to me on demand. Your personal cogitations are neither needed nor desired. This is school!"

I will allow that this is an extreme case and that most teachers and other educators of youth are not so blunt. Yet in more subtle ways, this is exactly the message that many of the older generation have communicated to the developing minds and morals of the younger one. If we do not really value thinking for oneself, we will not be able to transmit this one value that makes possible the acquisition of all others.

John Gardner said it well: "All too often we are giving our young people cut flowers when we should be teaching them to grow their own plants. We are stuffing their heads with earlier innovation rather than teaching them to innovate. We think of the mind as a storehouse to be filled when we should be thinking of it as an instrument to be used." [16]

"Someone has said that the last act of a dying organization is to get out a new and enlarged edition of the rule book." [17]

"Instead of giving young people the impression that their task is to stand a dreary watch over the ancient values, we should be telling them . . . that it is their task to re-create those values continuously in their own behavior, facing the dilemmas and catastrophes of their own time." [18]

To what does this lead us? Just this: I cannot be a whole person if I live by the values imposed by other people or by my culture unless I can honestly embrace those values as my own. The poet-philosopher Goethe once wrote, "What thou has inherited from thy fathers, acquire it to make it thine." No greater challenge faces us as parents, teachers, and leaders of youth than to aid our young people in this acquiring process that the worthwhile values of the fathers might truly become the *personal* property of the sons and daughters.

Notes

[1] Viktor Frankl, *From Death Camp to Existentialism* (Boston: Beacon Press, 1959), pp. 65, 66.

[2] May, *Man's Search*, pp. 160, 161.

[3] *Ibid.*, p. 163.

[4] *Ibid.*, p. 168, 169.

[5] White, *Education*, p. 288.

[6] *Ibid.*, p. 17.

[7] *Ibid.*, p. 18.

[8] ———, *The Ministry of Healing* (Mountain View, Calif.: Pacific Press Pub. Assn., 1942), p. 386.

[9] May, *op. cit.*, p. 217.

[10] *Ibid.*, p. 219.

[11] *Ibid.*, p. 220, 221.

[12] *Ibid.*, p. 209.

[13] *Ibid.*, p. 230.

[14] *Ibid.*, p. 225.

[15] White, *Education*, p. 230. (Italics supplied.)

[16] John W. Gardner, *Self-renewal* (New York: Harper and Row, 1963), pp. 21, 22.

[17] *Ibid.*, p. 45.

[18] *Ibid.*, p. 126.

CHAPTER 8

Anatomy of a Value

Students of human anatomy learn the various components of the body. They study the muscles, the bones, the skin, the organs, and the blood vessels. They discover that the brain is composed of 12 billion nerve cells. They know the makeup of the human organism. But what does a value look like?

In an earlier chapter I noted that a value can be defined not only by its content but by the process through which it is acquired. In chapter 6 we looked at the importance of content as we considered the best or most fundamental values. Here I wish to explore the other side of the coin. For purposes of value transmission the *process* (How did the youth get it?) may be more helpful than the *product* (What did the youth get?). One of the best-known descriptions of the process of valuing has been given by Louis Raths and associates.[1] They present seven criteria of a value, organized under the three headings of *choosing, prizing,* and *acting.*

Choosing

Choice is the essential bedrock of valuing, as we saw in the previous chapter. Without choice, desirable behaviors may be present, but no values. Three criteria come under this heading.

The first is *choosing freely.* "Choose for yourselves this day whom you will serve" (Joshua 24:15). Coercion is ruled out. Values cannot be imposed upon one by outside pressures.

Suppose we visit the campus of an Adventist boarding academy on a Sabbath morning. We observe the students, neatly dressed in their churchgoing garb, file into the chapel and take their seats for the worship service. We conclude that church attendance is certainly a value with this group of adolescents. But then we learn that being present and on time for the religious meetings is required at this school and that students who "skip out" will be punished. Now we are no longer certain whether church attendance is a value with these young people. We will not know until they are free of the constraints of authority. Then will they choose to attend on their own?

Please notice that I am not discussing the rightness or wrongness of requiring church attendance. Several good reasons may be advanced for this practice. But it does not constitute a value on the part of the young person, nor will being forced to go make him/her more likely to attend later on after the authority is no longer present. To think otherwise is to fool ourselves.

This raises the question of whether or not children and teenagers should always be free to choose. The answer is Of course not. Choice may be withheld because the results are too dangerous—such as playing in the street; smoking marijuana; riding in a car filled with drinking, irresponsible teenagers; or single dating late at night in an automobile. Or choice may be denied because it interferes with the rights and needs of others—such as the youth smoking or playing loud rock music in the parental home or engaging in activities that drain the parental treasury. Then too, it may be desirable to preserve a certain climate or atmosphere in a home or school—such as shared religious services or the absence of indiscreet public displays of affection.

However, all these reasons must stand on their own merits and not be offered as rationalizations for moral education. We should be open with a young person about situations in which we are not willing to offer a choice. And we should explain why as clearly as possible. But when we are concerned with value development, we must be willing to give a child his freedom to choose. For only in free choice, without fear of reprisal, are values formed.

The second mark of a value is *choosing from alternatives*. Suppose that I go to an ice-cream counter and ask what flavors the store has today. The young lady with the white apron tells me that she is out of everything but vanilla. After pondering the situation for a few moments, I reply, "I'll take vanilla." Would you conclude that vanilla is a favorite ice cream for me? Hardly!

Where one has no real alternatives, no actual choice exists; hence, no value is being formed. That is why God placed the forbidden tree in the Garden of Eden (Genesis 3). Adam and Eve could not choose obedience to God as their highest value unless they also had the opportunity to choose disobedience. If they were to become truly principled people, a means of rejecting God's claims must be provided. Some people are good simply because they have lacked the opportunity to be bad.

Years ago, when I was serving as a ministerial intern, my senior pastor and I were invited to a meeting of clergymen of the various churches in our city. The meeting was to include a noon luncheon, so upon arrival I slipped into the kitchen and explained that we were vegetarians. The hosts very graciously assured me that they would meet our needs.

At midday we sat around long tables while the luncheon plates were placed before us. Most contained roast beef. But then the servers appeared with *three* very attractive vegetarian plates—for my colleague and me and for a minister of another denomination who was sitting beside us. I sensed a mistake and wondered what would happen next. The gentleman studied his plate and finally, in a good-natured way, said something like "We vegetarians have to stick together."

At this my senior pastor perked up his ears and inquired, "Oh, how long have you been a vegetarian?"

"I just started" was the quick rejoinder.

His "value" of vegetarianism was explained by the lack of a convenient alternative.

Sometimes what seems to be an alternative is not actually one at all, or is so unpalatable that no true choice exists. I cannot really say that I value eating, since the only alternative is starving to death, although I can value some foods over others. If I tell a child that he can behave a certain way or take a beating with a belt, I have not really extended a choice. Recently, a judge asked a convicted murderer if he would prefer being executed by the firing squad or by hanging. Those are not the kinds of alternatives that will demonstrate a value. If all the alternatives are grim, no "choice" occurs in the sense that we have been using the word. The youth must have at least one alternative that he/she considers desirable for any value formation to take place.

The third criterion of a value is *choosing after thoughtful consideration of the consequences of each alternative.* "Suppose a king is about to go to war against another king. Will he not first sit down and consider whether he is able with ten thousand men to oppose the one coming against him with twenty thousand? If he is not able, he will send a delegation while the other is still a long way off and will ask for terms of peace. In the same way, any of you who does not give up everything he has cannot be my disciple" (Luke 14:31-33).

Even if a choice has been freely made from genuine alternatives, no valuing occurs unless it was an informed choice—based on evidence. Suppose I offer a 4-year-old a reward. "Would you like this bright, shiny quarter in my right hand or this dirty, old, crumpled $20 bill in my left?" She takes the quarter. What does that prove? Only that she has no understanding of the worth of the alternatives. The choice is made in ignorance. No genuine values are present.

Under peer pressure a boy chooses to take up smoking. He has no comprehension of the consequences. What does he know of lung cancer and emphysema? He has never experienced such suffering or observed it at close hand in others. Genuine values are not operating here. A girl compromises her morals in a moment of passion. She cannot visualize the meaning of an abortion with its accompanying guilt, or the anguish of raising a fatherless child alone, or the emptiness of a forced marriage. And both of these teenagers never thought that these things would happen to *them*. So their choices do not reveal values as internalized principles, since they were not made in the full knowledge of what they were choosing.

The first three criteria, each involving an aspect of choice, represent the cognitive or thinking processes of valuing. They call for the use of the mind. They tell us that value education must have a rational foundation. The next group represents the affective or feeling processes of valuing. They tell us that value education also has an emotional component.

Prizing

The fourth characteristic of a value is *prizing and cherishing*. When we value something, we esteem it and hold it dear. We are happy with our values. "Oh, how I love your law!" wrote the psalmist. "I meditate on it all day long" (Ps. 119:97).

It is possible to choose freely and thoughtfully and yet not be happy with our choice. We do something we would rather not, as when one chooses the least objectionable of several undesirable alternatives. A person may volunteer time on a Sabbath afternoon to go from door to door passing out missionary literature because he feels it is his duty, when he hates the assignment and would rather be almost anywhere else. Many Christians are miserable in their faith but hang on out of a sense of guilt or a fear of punishment. These choices cannot be called genuine values.

An excellent biblical illustration is the older brother in the parable Jesus told of the lost son. When the prodigal came home, the older brother was angry and accused the forgiving father: "Look! All these years I've been slaving for you and never disobeyed your orders. Yet you never gave me even a young goat so I could celebrate with my friends. But when this son of yours who has squandered your property with prostitutes comes home, you kill the fattened calf for him!" (Luke 15:29, 30).

What an insight we are given into his value system. Sure, he stayed on the farm like a good boy while his brother lived it up. But he wasn't happy about it. He considered it drudgery. He found no joy in his father's companionship. He thought his brother was the one really having fun. But he stayed with an eye on the reward. And now was this wastrel to be cut back in? Was he to eat his cake and have it too? Don't look for values here. Genuine values must be rejoiced in, respected, celebrated.

The fifth criterion of a value is *affirming publicly*. When we value something, we are proud of it. We don't try to hide it. We are not embarrassed by it. "If anyone is ashamed of me and my words, the Son of Man will be ashamed of him when he comes in his glory" (chap. 9:26). A "secret Christian" is a contradiction in terms.

An old story tells about a young believer who spent a summer working in a northern logging camp. When he returned, a friend asked how he, as a Christian, had gotten along among the rough and profane men in that restricted setting. "It was no problem," he answered. "They never found out I was a Christian."

If I really value something, I want you to know. I may be tactful so as not to come on as "pushy," but I look for ways to share with you what is so important to me. Part of God's plan for our salvation is that "you confess with your mouth, 'Jesus is Lord' " (Rom. 10:9). A value-affirming theme may well be "I'll tell the world that I'm a Christian."

Acting

If the first set of criteria is concerned with cognitive processes and the second set with emotions and feelings, the third set is behavioral in nature. The sixth distinctive mark of a value is *acting upon choices*. Here is where "the rubber meets the road." The first five criteria could be present and the whole thing consist of just talk—head religion! Now comes the time, as they say, to "put your money where your mouth is."

If helping people is part of our value system, we will give of our time and energies to help. If we believe in the church, we will open up our wallets and support its programs with our money. If the Christian home is important to us, we will treat our spouses and children with love and kindness. If we affirm the dignity and brother-hood of all humanity, we will work for equal status for all peoples and will refrain from ethnic slurs and jokes. If we believe war is wrong, we will strive for peace. How we spend our time, our treasure, and our energies provides an important clue to our value system. The person who talks about something but never does anything about it only *thinks* he has a value. "Not everyone who says to me, 'Lord, Lord,' will enter the kingdom of heaven, but only he who does the will of my Father who is in heaven" (Matt. 7:21).

The seventh criterion of a value is *repeating*. Valuing is not a one-shot effort. The person who gives a large offering to missions following a fervent appeal but who never gives anything thereafter does not hold missions in high value. Things we value show up in our behavior in different situations and at different times. They are persistent and pervasive. They establish a pattern in living. We cannot be holy people on the Sabbath and profane the rest of the week. We must take our values into the workshop, the office, the marketplace, and the home.

A person may be tempted to think that because he once held a value, he still does. One way to check is to evaluate the pattern of living. Do I still read my Bible as much as I used to? Does my daily conversation contain anything about my faith in Jesus? Have my offerings to the church kept up with inflation? When was the last time I went out of my way to help anyone? "He who stands firm to the end will be saved" (chap. 24:13).

It becomes clear that the criteria for a value as we have

been defining it is rather stringent. It is also clear that some things resembling values do not quite make the grade. Raths and his associates call these "value indicators." [2] They include (1) goals or purposes, (2) aspirations, (3) attitudes, (4) interests, (5) feelings, (6) beliefs and convictions, (7) activities, and (8) worries, problems, and obstacles. These do not necessarily meet all the criteria for a value in themselves. But they are indicators of possible values. By using methods to be described later in this book, we may elevate them to the level of a value.

This, then, is the process of acquiring a value or a value system. By combining this process with the product of cosmic, overarching, universal, relational religious values, we may gain a vision of what we as parents, teachers, and leaders of youth should be transmitting. We now turn to the topic of just *how* this transmission takes place.

Notes

[1] Raths et al., *Values and Teaching*, pp. 27-48.
[2] *Ibid.*, pp. 30-33.

How Values Are Acquired

CHAPTER 9

Values Transmission: A Bird's-eye View

One of the earliest studies of values employing scientific research methods was conducted back in the 1920s. The Character Education Inquiry shocked the educational world and is still widely cited today. Sponsored by Teachers College, Columbia University, the report was written by Hugh Hartshorne and Mark May and presented in four books bound in two volumes. The researchers tested eleven thousand children, ages 8 to 16, in the areas of deceit, service, and self-control. It was truly a massive and thorough study. A review of its major findings will be a good starting place in our search for the "how" of values transmission.

The Character Education Inquiry

Three measures of deceit—cheating, lying, and stealing—were employed. The youth were placed in situations where they were given opportunity to practice deception without any seeming possibility of getting caught. However, the tasks were rigged so that the researchers could tell who had cheated, lied, or stolen and who had not. The results?

"The concomitants of deceit are, in order of their importance, (1) classroom association; (2) general personal handicaps, such as relatively low IQ, poor resistance to suggestion, and emotional stability; (3) cultural and social limitations in the home background." [1]

Notice the emphasis on environmental influences. "Deceit is associated with such factors as parental discord, parental example, bad discipline, unsocial attitude toward the children, impoverished type of community, and changing social or economic situation." [2] The theme of parental unity and harmony will come up again and again when more recent research studies are examined.

The report is also significant for what it *didn't* find. "There is no relation . . . between Sunday school attendance and deception. . . . Children who attend regularly cheat . . . about the same as those who rarely or never attend." [3] This was disquieting news to religious educators, for it established that direct religious instruction has little influence on moral behavior. We will need to keep this in mind as we plan for the most effective methods of values education.

Perhaps even more unsettling was the finding that moral behavior does not transfer well from one situation to another. "Neither deceit nor . . . 'honesty' are unified character traits, but rather specific functions of life situations. Most children will deceive in certain situations and not in others." [4]

"No one is honest or dishonest by 'nature,'" the authors explain. Where a conflict arises between a child and his environment, he will try to gain his ends in any way possible. If deceitful ways are successful in accomplishing this, they will continue, "unless definite training is undertaken through which direct and honest methods may also become successful." [5]

Preaching high values is simply not effective. "The mere urging of honest behavior by teachers or the discussion of standards and ideals of honesty, no matter how much such general ideals may be 'emotionalized,' has no necessary relation to the control of conduct." [6] What should we do, then?

"The main attention of educators should be placed not so much on devices for teaching honesty or any other 'trait' as on the reconstruction of school practices in such a way as to provide not occasional but consistent and regular opportunities for the successful use by both teachers and pupils of such forms of conduct as make for the common good." [7]

When the researchers turn their attention to the area of service and unselfishness, much the same situation prevails. As in studies of deceit, "such efforts to train children in forms of charitable and cooperative behavior as are ordinarily used in school have very little, if any, effect." [8]

"The most important factor in determining the service behavior is the mutual friendship of children in the same classroom. Next in significance is satisfactory school adjustment. . . . Third is the influence of the home . . . as shown by the resemblance of siblings, the effect of parental example, and such cultural factors as are bound up with occupational level, treatment of children, knowledge of etiquette and general cultural information, and good habits in the care of one's body." [9]

The various lines of evidence all seem to point to a warm, caring, mutually supportive climate as the laboratory in which appropriate values are best developed. Lawrence Kohlberg reports that recent findings on children agree with Hartshorne and May that resistance to temptation is related more to *situational* factors than to a fixed moral character trait. He summarizes the evidence as:

1. Cheating in one situation has low predictability for cheating in another.

2. Youth are not divisible into "cheaters" and "non-cheaters," but are normally distributed around a mean of moderate cheating.

3. The tendency to cheat depends on the risk of detection.

4. Peer group approval and example is important in determining honest behavior. [10]

Hartshorne and May found no relationship between behavioral tests of honesty or service and exposure to Sunday schools, Scouts, or character education classes. Kohlberg notes that four more recent studies found no positive or consistent relationship between earliness and amount of parental demands or training in good habits and measures of children's obedience, responsibility, and honesty.[11] If direct instruction and discipline measures do not seem to produce results, what might be the key to unlock the door to effective values education?

Philosophies of Moral Development

Theories of moral development may be generally related to three philosophical doctrines of the nature of man.[12] The first is that mankind is basically sinful and corrupt. Children are naturally evil with antisocial impulses that must be redirected. While this was the position of the medieval church and still influences contemporary religious thought, the doctrine in the twentieth century has been best captured in a secular thought system—psychoanalysis.

Psychoanalysis would define morality as the need to keep antisocial impulses from conscious awareness. Thus we see a reality-sensitive ego trying to suppress or repress a self-gratifying, aggressive id to keep harmony with a set of parental principles that have become internalized (superego). Because of the complexity of this theory and its paucity of practical applications, we shall not discuss it further.

The second doctrine is that mankind is innately good but that the child is corrupted by society. The modern philosophy of moral development based on this doctrine is the cognitive development approach of Jean Piaget and those who have followed his lead. A moral act is defined as one that is based on conscious prior judgment of its rightness or wrongness. Strategies for facilitating moral development are those that emphasize various stages of development in advancing age groups and the cognitive changes associated with each stage. Because of its rich explanatory power and the many practical strategies associated with it, we will spend considerable time with this philosophy.

The third doctrine states that the newborn infant is

neither corrupt nor pure but malleable—a tabula rasa, or blank tablet, on which we may write whatever we choose. In the twentieth century this doctrine is encapsulated in learning theory. Morality is defined as specific acts or avoidances that are learned on the basis of rewards and punishments. Strategies for transmitting values are mainly composed of adult socialization techniques, sometimes called "social learning." Since both research and common observation support learning theory, I will devote considerable space to it.

It is important to note that we will consider what these theories can teach us without regard to the doctrine of man in which they may be rooted. Most Adventists would probably not accept any of these doctrines in their purest form but would find the truth in some combination of them.

Ellen White writes: "A perception of right, a desire for goodness, exists in every heart. But against these principles there is struggling an antagonistic power. The result of the eating of the tree of knowledge of good and evil is manifest in every man's experience. There is in his nature a bent to evil, a force which, unaided, he cannot resist. To withstand this force, to attain that ideal which in his inmost soul he accepts as alone worthy, he can find help in but one power. That power is Christ." [13]

Here we see in man a mixture of good and evil that is also reflected in Scripture (Romans 7). These theories also present other problems. For example, learning theory, carried to its extreme, would deny free will, for we are supposedly merely the products of our environment. Therefore, it is important at this juncture to make clear that I do not endorse any of the moral development theories in their entirety. Nevertheless, there is some truth in each one. It is my purpose to dig out these truths and the practical suggestions that arise out of them. All of this I propose to set forth within a Christian framework. What we want to know is how we can use the explanations of theorists and the findings of behavioral scientists to inculcate values that strengthen our relationships and those of our children with God and with our fellow humans.

Internalization of Moral Standards

Each approach to moral development, regardless of how it may differ from other approaches, is concerned with the internalization of moral standards—what Freud called the "superego" and Durkeim the "collective conscience." Hoffman explains: "The individual does not go through life viewing society's central norms as externally and coercively imposed pressures to which he must submit. Though the norms are initially alien, they are eventually adopted by the individual, largely through the efforts of his early social- izers—the parents—and come to serve as internalized guides so that he behaves in accord with them even when external authority is not present to enforce them. That is, control by others is replaced by self-control." [14]

Of course, this process has its limits. External surveil- lance may remove much of the necessity for it (no opportunity to learn to think for yourself), the larger social system may counteract parental influence (peers or voca- tional environment, for example), or internalized values may collapse under social pressure (as in the Milgram research). But all of this does not negate the importance of internalization.

Internalization may be defined as acts that are free from subjective concerns about external sanctions. [15] That is, the person is not motivated by fear of what people or supernatural forces might do. The behavior may be triggered by an external stimulus (such as stopping at a traffic light) unless that stimulus raises fear of detection (reminds one that a policeman may be watching). Internal- ized behavior can be based on positive attitudes toward an absent reference figure (I admire my father's honesty and want to be like him) but not on fear of punishment from that figure if deviant behavior was discovered.

Three levels toward internalization may be listed:

1. Individual has a conditioned fear or anxiety that results from repeated punishment. This is only borderline internalization.

2. Individual has a positive orientation toward an absent reference group or person.

3. Individual experiences the standards as an obligation to himself rather than to some outside reference figure.[16]

How to move a young person to the highest level as we transmit our religious values will be the purpose of our search as we examine the theories of moral development more carefully.

Notes

[1] Hugh Hartshorne and Mark May, *Studies in the Nature of Character* (New York: Macmillan Company, 1928-1929), vol. 1, p. 412.

[2] *Ibid.*, p. 409.

[3] *Ibid.*, p. 411.

[4] *Ibid.*

[5] *Ibid.*, p. 412.

[6] *Ibid.*, p. 413.

[7] *Ibid.*, p. 414.

[8] *Ibid.*, vol. 2, p. 273.

[9] *Ibid.*, p. 272.

[10] Lawrence Kohlberg, "Development of Moral Character and Moral Ideology," in Martin Hoffman and Lois Hoffman, eds., *Review of Child Development Research* (New York: Russell Sage Foundation, 1964), vol. 1, p. 386.

[11] *Ibid.*, p. 388.

[12] Martin L. Hoffman, "Moral Development," in *Carmichael's Manual of Child Psychology*, 3d ed. (New York: John Wiley and Sons, 1970), vol. 2, pp. 261, 262.

[13] White, *Education*, p. 29.

[14] Hoffman, "Moral Development," p. 262.

[15] *Ibid.*, pp. 263, 264.

[16] *Ibid.*

CHAPTER 10

Moral Judgment: A Cognitive View

Does religion have anything to do with intellect? Can a "thinking" Christian serve God better? Is mental development related to values formation? Or is simple trust, with mind in neutral, enough? Morality may be viewed from several different perspectives. One is how well the person measures up to behavioral criteria such as resistance to temptation. This was the approach taken by Hartshorne and May, as noted in the previous chapter. A second is the extent to which a person experiences the emotion of guilt when violating a standard. This is a basic motive for morality in both psychoanalytic and learning theory.

A third perspective may be called judgmental. Morality is defined as the capacity to make judgments in terms of a standard and to justify maintaining the standard to oneself and to others. This is the approach taken by Jean Piaget and by Lawrence Kohlberg. Because this approach is basic to much that has been researched and written in the field of moral development and because it is rather complex, we will spend some time trying to simplify it and put it into a framework for the transmission of Christian values.

The Cognitive Stages of Piaget

The cognitive-developmental approach was first suggested by the work of John Dewey. According to Kohlberg and Elsa Wasserman it is "called *cognitive* because it recognized that moral education, like intellectual education, has its basis in stimulating the *active thinking* of the child about moral issues and decisions." The *developmental* part means that it "sees the aims of moral education as movements through moral stages." [1]

In this perspective a close connection exists between moral development and mental maturity. "Advanced moral reasoning depends on advanced logical reasoning. A person's logical stage puts a certain ceiling on the moral stage he or she can attain." However, "most individuals are higher in logical stage than they are in moral stage." [2]

The Swiss psychologist Jean Piaget carefully studied the development of the thinking processes in children and concluded that they pass through a series of stages that are age-related. Little children mostly respond to the stimuli in their environment rather than think. But by about 6 years the child is able to do concrete mental operations. Not until about age 11 is the youth able to do abstract, or "formal operational," thinking. Some adults remain at the concrete operational stage all their lives.

It is outside the scope of this book to give detailed descriptions of Piaget's intellectual stages, since we are interested primarily in values transmission. We cite them only as a basis for the moral stages that are built upon them. What happens in the transformation from concrete operational to formal operational thought is pertinent. Scharf and his associates explain: "Instead of considering only single explanations of phenomena or single solutions to problems, children begin to weigh possibilities and to select from a number of alternatives. They begin to be able to judge friends, relatives, and peers from vantage points other than their own." [3]

Piaget early saw that these were the very qualities necessary to principled thinking and set forth a corresponding series of moral stages. I will follow Hoffman's comprehensive review. [4] For Piaget, morality is (1) respect for the rules of social order and (2) a sense of justice (concern for reciprocity and equality among individuals). He postulated a developmental shift in the relative strength of these two aspects—from respect and submission to authority toward self-government and self-control.

Below the age of 6, children are basically egocentric, and therefore amoral, but from approximately 6 to 10 years of age they are in stage 1, which Piaget called "morality of constraint" or "heteronomous morality." The distinguishing marks are:

1. An obligation to obey rules because they are sacred and unalterable.

2. The judging of behaviors as totally right or totally wrong—no gray areas.

3. The magnitude of the consequences as the determination of the rightness or wrongness of an act (accidentally dropping a whole stack of dishes is naughtier than deliberately breaking one plate).

4. Whether an act conforms exactly to the rules and/or whether it elicits punishment.

5. The concept of "imminent justice"—violations of a rule are followed by misfortunes that are construed as punishments.

To illustrate the latter point: When I was a stage 1 boy, I spent a few days visiting favorite relatives in the big city. My cousin excitedly announced that her parents had purchased tickets for all of us to attend the circus—on Sabbath! I knew I shouldn't go, but as the only Adventist in the group, I didn't know how to tell them. They were doing something special for me, and I was just a kid—so I went with much trepidation. That night I became violently sick to my stomach. I was certain that God was punishing me, although more mature reflection suggests that it might well have been my guilt combined with the circus hot dogs I had forced down myself during the entertainment.

From about 11 years on up, children enter stage 2, which Piaget called "autonomous morality," "morality of cooperation," or "reciprocity." During this stage:

1. Rules are established and maintained through reciprocal social agreement and thus are subject to modification in response to human needs or other situational demands.

2. Diversity in views of right and wrong, rather than moral absolutism, is seen as possible.

3. Right and wrong are determined not simply by the consequences of an act but by the motives and intention to deceive.

4. Punishment is not impersonally ordained. Natural consequences exist. Punishment should be reciprocally related to the misdeed.

5. Duty and obligation, rather than being merely obedience to authority, are more likely to revolve around (a) peer expectations, (b) gratitude for past affection and favors, and (c) above all, putting oneself in the place of others.

Numerous studies have shown these stages to be positively related to age. That is, children cannot be expected to reason morally at a higher level than their chronological maturity. However, just because young people attain the necessary age, it does not follow that they automatically adopt stage 2 morality. How does a child move between the stages? Piaget felt that both maturation and the right type of experience play a role. Experience involves interaction with peers (and with parents if they interact in ways that foster moral growth). The process usually takes the following steps:

1. The child shares in making decisions and thus gains a new conception of rules. The rules are not simply dropped down from above.

2. The child takes alternate and reciprocal roles with others.

3. The child learns to judge by intentions rather than simply by outward actions.

The process of "interactionism" is described by Jack Fraenkel:

"As the child grows and matures, however, she undergoes experiences for which her previously developed cognitive structure is inadequate. She thus seeks to revamp her way of thinking in order to make sense of the new experience. When she finds a new way of thinking that enables her to understand the experience, her cognitive structure—her way of thinking about the world—is changed accordingly. An essential ingredient for . . . the cognitie development of the child . . . , therefore, is the opportunity to engage in a number of new and different experiences that will cause her to try to reorder her way of thinking and to seek out more adequate ways to organize and interpret data." [5]

Kohlberg's Extension of Piaget

Kohlberg and his associates have conducted many interviews with adolescents. A particularly noteworthy study was the interviewing of fifty Chicago-area boys between the ages of 10 and 16, who were then reinterviewed at three-year intervals over a twenty-year period.[6] Each subject was asked to respond to ten moral dilemmas in which acts of obedience to laws or rules conflict with the needs or welfare of other persons. The youth was asked what action the character in the story should take in view of the moral dilemma. Then a series of questions probed *why* the youth felt that that particular action was appropriate. The level of moral maturity is determined not by the choice of action but by the type of reasoning behind that choice.

As a result of his research Kohlberg has proposed six stages of moral development arranged into three levels of moral orientation.[7] Since these are fundamental to this whole approach, let us examine them carefully.

The first level is the premoral or preconventional orientation. Here the control of conduct is external both as to the standards themselves and as to the motivation for obeying them. The child evaluates behavior on the basis of physical or hedonistic consequences. The level is divided into two stages.

Stage 1 is the punishment and obedience orientation. Motivation for behavior is to avoid punishment or to obey a superior power unquestioningly. This is the beginning of moral judgment, and all children commence here. Hopefully they will move on to more mature and principled reasons for good behavior. But some never do. What about the adult who carefully obeys the traffic laws so that he won't receive a ticket for speeding? Stage 1 reasoning. Or in a religious context: "I couldn't go through life with all those do's and don'ts. But I guess I have to if I want to go to heaven." [8] The chief motivation of some Christians for doing the right thing is to escape hell.

Stage 2 is the instrumental relativist orientation. Motivation for behavior is to satisfy one's own needs and sometimes those of others if they will reward one in return. It is a step up from stage 1 in that it is not done through fear, but it is just as self-centered and selfish. What's in it for me? is the predominant question. In religion it comes out as: "It pays to serve Jesus." "Give a faithful tithe, and you'll prosper even when tornados are destroying the neighbors' property and economic collapse is sending others to the poorhouse." "Endure a little suffering here so you can revel in milk and honey in the great by-and-by."

Note that under either of these stages, the behavior may be perfectly good (or it may not be). The determining factor for moral maturity is not what you do but *why you do it*. One can do good things for poor reasons or do things not good in themselves but for highly principled reasons. However, motivation, under this model of morality, does not divide neatly into a dichotomy of "good" and "bad" reasons. Rather, it lies on a continuum from less to greater moral maturity.

The second level is the conventional orientation. Behavior is based on conforming to and maintaining the conventional social order. What is right is determined largely by what others say is right. Control of conduct is external as to standards set by others, but motivation is largely internal as the child takes the role of significant others. As the name suggests, most adults operate on this level. It also is divided into two stages.

Stage 3 is the "good boy—nice girl" orientation. Behavior is motivated by the desire to please others and gain their approval. What will they think of me? becomes the important question. A man may be polite, gracious, and pious at church but a raging tyrant at home. Or maybe his church behavior goes home with him because he wants even his family to think well of him. I may give a large donation to the church-building project or work at the Community Services center, ministering to the poor, or even volunteer for foreign mission service—all to build my reputation. Is that why Jesus said, "When you give to the needy, do not let your left hand know what your right hand is doing" (Matt. 6:3)? Morality is deeply embedded in motivation.

Stage 4 is the law and order orientation. Good behavior consists of respecting authority, doing one's duty, and maintaining the given social order for its own sake. At this stage law (divine or human) is important, but it is applied without regard for its effects on people. In religion it may produce eye-for-an-eye-and-tooth-for-a-tooth mentality, like that of the Pharisees of Jesus' day. If a stage 4 person had been present when the woman taken in adultery (John 8:2-11) was brought before Him, he would probably have said, "Stone her!" because that's how the law read. Stage 4 people would not break laws even though they might be unjust and oppressive. They would not have signed up as conductors on the pre-Civil War Underground Railroad.

This discussion is in no way intended to belittle the concept of law. Both divine and human law is vital to moral behavior. It does call into question *legalism*—the keeping of law for its own sake, regardless of how it serves God and people. Even here, though, law and order morality is on a more mature level than the first three stages. But there are heights yet to be attained.

The third level is the postconventional, autonomous, or principled orientation. At this level, one makes a clear effort to define moral values and principles that have validity and application apart from the authority of the groups or persons holding these principles. We might say that these values are self-authenticating. The control of conduct is internal, for the standards have the internal source of an enlightened conscience, and the motivation to act is based upon an inner process of thought and judgment. This level is divided into the final two stages.

Stage 5 is the social contract orientation. Laws or rules are seen to have a rational basis; that is, they express the will of the majority, maximize social utility or welfare, or are necessary for institutional functioning. Moral behavior is viewed as that which is best for the majority of the people. The individual tries to keep from violating the rights or denying the needs of others. This is the "official" morality of the United States Constitution. It may be represented by a Christian family holding a council to decide on standards for the home. Each member has input, and each respects the position and feelings of all others.

Stage 6 is the universal ethical principle orientation. Right is defined by the decision of the conscience in accord with self-chosen ethical principles appealing to logical comprehensiveness, universality, and consistency. These principles are based on justice and fairness for everyone, a respect for the dignity of all human beings, and mutual trust. The principles are abstract rather than specific. An excellent example is the golden rule: "In everything, do to others what you would have them do to you, for this sums up the Law and the Prophets" (Matt. 7:12). Another is Kant's categorical imperative: "Act only on that maxim which will enable you at the same time to will that it be a universal law."

Stage 6 people do what is right according to their inner ideals regardless of the reactions of others in their immediate environment. The only punishment they fear is the self-condemnation of failing to be true to themselves. It goes without saying that few mortals have reached this pinnacle. It is illustrated most perfectly by Jesus Christ Himself.

Turiel conducted an experimental study to test several Kohlberg hypotheses. He found that the six stages are successively advanced cognitive levels, and children are more likely to progress from one to the next than to leapfrog any of them. Further, the experience of cognitive conflict (different points of view expressed by the experimenter) may be an important factor in moral development.

On the other hand, he found only weak support for "irreversibility"—the phenomenon of a push toward forward movement and resistance against backward movement. In truth, most people do not always operate at one level but move back and forth in various situations. [9]

Kohlberg believes we can aid our children in moving to higher levels by confronting them with moral reasoning one stage above the one in which they are primarily operating at the current time. We will consider how to do this in a chapter in the third section of the book. But first we turn to examine the stages more closely.

Notes

[1] Lawrence Kohlberg and Elsa Wasserman, "The Cognitive-Developmental Approach and the Practicing Counselor," *The Personnel and Guidance Journal* 58 (May, 1980): 560.

[2] *Ibid.*, p. 561.

[3] Peter Scharf, William McCoy, and Diane Ross, *Growing Up Moral: Dilemmas for the Intermediate Grades* (Minneapolis: Winston Press, 1979), p. 12.

[4] Hoffman, "Moral Development," pp. 265-270.

[5] Fraenkel, *How to Teach About Values*, p. 59.

[6] Kohlberg and Wasserman, *op. cit.*, p. 561.

[7] *Ibid.*, p. 562; Hoffman, *op. cit.*, pp. 276, 277.

[8] Dudley, *Why Teenagers Reject Religion*, p. 17.

[9] Hoffman, *op.cit.*, pp. 279, 280.

CHAPTER 11

All the World's a Stage

Young people attending parochial schools, where they receive daily religious instruction, will be higher up the ladder of moral maturity than other youth who are not so privileged, wouldn't you think? So did Derrick Proctor when he set out to study 415 seniors at nine Seventh-day Adventist high schools in four Midwestern states. Proctor used three of Kohlberg's moral dilemmas and assigned a moral maturity score to each student. His purpose was to look for relationships between moral maturity and several other variables. What he *really* discovered eclipsed everything else and became the major finding of his research.

Adolescents in this study demonstrated a relatively low level of moral maturity when compared with subjects in other studies, not only of the same age but also of younger ages. While other research using subjects of similar ages usually finds all stages from 1 to 5 represented, 42 percent of Proctor's subjects were at stage 2 and 58 percent at stage 3. Only one student was at stage 4. Comparing the findings with those of about two dozen other studies, Proctor concluded that his subjects were four to five years behind other youth in the same socioeconomic class as to moral maturity. They were less frequently at stage 1 but did not seem to advance to stages 4 or 5.

How can this be? Proctor surmised that (1) this may be in line with some studies that show conservatism of religious beliefs to be associated with lower moral maturity scores, (2) a more conservative Midwest may have introduced a geographical factor, and (3) adults who had generally lower moral development might have been their parents and teachers.[1]

Please notice that the Proctor research does *not* demonstrate that the behavior of Adventist teenagers is less moral than that of other youth. In some ways it was undoubtedly better. What is in question here are the reasons for the behavior. Perhaps as parents and teachers we have focused so strongly on the correct behavior that we have not helped the youth internalize the principles on which it should be based.

"All the world's a stage," exclaimed Shakespeare. He could have been talking about moral development, for every moral judgment that each of us makes is from the framework of one of the six stages. Let us examine a bit more closely the kind of thinking that qualifies one for higher-stage morality.

A Closer Look at the Moral Stages

Moral character is believed to result from strength of ego or *will*.[2] Morality is based on consideration of how one's action affects others and consideration of how it affects the self's long-range interests. Particular aspects of this ego strength are:

1. General intelligence.

2. The tendency to anticipate future events and choose a greater, but remote, outcome over a lesser immediate outcome.

3. Capacity to maintain stable, focused attention.

4. Capacity to control unsocial fantasies.

5. Self-esteem, or satisfaction with self and environment.

Mature moral judgment contains a number of aspects that are developmental; that is, they increase with maturity. We cannot expect young children to start at the higher stages. Advanced moral reasoning is simply incomprehensible to them. The ladder of mature moral reasoning must be climbed round by round. Some of these developmental aspects are:

1. *Intentionality in judgment:* Younger children judge goodness or badness by the actual consequences of an act, while older ones are able to consider intent. They know the difference between breaking cups while helping mother or while trying to steal the jam.

2. *Relativism in judgment:* Younger children see an act as totally wrong or totally right, while older ones can appreciate a conflict of views and see various perspectives.

3. *Independence of sanctions:* Younger children judge an act bad if it is punished, while older ones realize that a good act may be punished and a bad one go unpunished.

4. *Use of reciprocity:* A degree of maturity is necessary to be able to put oneself in another's place and view the situation from that person's perspective.

5. *Punishment as restitution:* Younger children are more likely to advocate severe punishment for another's misbehavior, while older ones are more likely to call for milder measures leading to reform.

6. *Naturalistic views of misfortune:* Less mature youth are more likely to think of misfortune as punishment willed by God.[3]

It is important to remember that chronological and physical development, while necessary for moral growth, do not by themselves assure it. Many adults are still in the more primitive stages of these aspects. It is well to compare this list with our own experience and with that of the youth to whom we hope to transmit our values.

But how does this moral movement look in terms of Kohlberg's six stages? Kohlberg has selected thirty-two aspects of morality. For each aspect he has suggested a specific stance that would define each of the six stages. To illustrate, I will look at just two of the aspects.

The first aspect is "motivation for rule obedience"— Why keep the rules? Stage 1 would obey the rules to avoid punishment. Stage 2 would obey to obtain rewards, have favors returned, et cetera. Stage 3 would obey to avoid disapproval or dislike by others. Stage 4 would obey to avoid censure by legitimate authorities with resultant guilt.

Stage 5 would obey to maintain the respect of the impartial spectator judging in terms of community welfare. Stage 6 would obey to avoid self-condemnation.[4]

The second (and more abstract) aspect of morality that I will illustrate is "the basis of moral worth of a human life." Stage 1 confuses the value of human life with the value of physical objects and bases its judgment on social status or physical attributes. Thus the strong, the beautiful, and the useful are worth more than the weak and ugly. Stage 2 sees human life as instrumental to the satisfaction of the needs of the possessor or others. Stage 3 bases its judgment on empathy and the affections of family members and others toward the possessor. Stage 4 conceives of life as sacred in terms of its place in a categorical moral or religious order of rights and duties. Stage 5 values life both in terms of relation to community welfare and in terms of life being a universal human right. Stage 6 believes in the sacredness of human life as representing a universal human value of respect for the individual.[5]

Moral Judgment Versus Moral Conduct

The work of Piaget and Kohlberg has been criticized[6] for stressing cognitive aspects of moral development to the point of ignoring affective considerations and for failing to explain what motivates the individual to try to make sense out of his experience and move forward rather than backward through the stages. We will deal with these considerations in the chapter on social learning.

The most serious criticism of these theorists, however, is that their data pertain to individual judgment of the actions of *others*. To what extent are notions of right and wrong and moral reasoning related to one's own moral behavior? In other words, does my ability to reason at the higher moral stages mean that my own conduct will be more moral? Kohlberg himself offers this comparison:

"Judgment does not appear to become "moral" until early adolescence, while "morality" of conduct appears to develop early. Individual differences in level of moral judgment are quite general and stable; morality of conduct is more specific to the situation and more unstable over time. Moral judgment appears to develop in the same direction regardless of social groups; moral conduct appears to develop in line with specific social class and peer-group norms." [7]

Fortunately, the two are not independent of each other. Moderately good correlations have been found in a number of studies. In the long run, neither is worth much without the other. While small children should be trained in proper behavior, right conduct without internalized values does not make a principled adolescent or adult. And the most advanced moral reasoning that is not backed up in the daily life is empty talk. Therefore parents have a twofold task: to facilitate the child's upward movement through the moral stages and to motivate the child to choose behavior in harmony with his/her highest ideals. Kohlberg defines moral maturity as "the capacity to make decisions and judgments which are moral [that is, based on internal principles] and to act in accordance with such judgments. While . . . the parent cannot escape the direct imposition of behavior demands and moral judgments upon the child, moral education is primarily a matter of stimulating the development of the child's own moral judgment and its control of action." [8]

What is it like in the higher stages? Scharf describes the principles of stages 5 and 6:

"These principles are seen as having validity apart from the authority of the group or individuals in power. The principled thinker is able to evaluate the moral validity of concrete social rules and norms by comparing them with more general ideals of justice and fairness.

Law is perceived as having a basis in consent and in the welfare of people rather than simply in a respect for authority, as at stage 4. Laws which aren't constitutional, which violate human rights, or which aren't in the general interest are judged invalid." [9]

In this connection, it may be helpful to introduce a

document written by Martin Luther King, Jr. "Letter From a Birmingham Jail" is one of the few statements available that Kohlberg has placed at stage 6. Fraenkel quotes it from King's book *Why We Can't Wait:*

"There is a type of constructive nonviolent tension which is necessary for growth. Just as Socrates felt it was necessary to create a tension in the mind so that individuals could rise from the bondage of half-truths, so must we see the need for nonviolent gadflies to create the kind of tension in society that will help men rise from the dark depths of prejudice and racism.

"One may well ask, 'How can you advocate breaking some laws and obeying others?' The answer lies in the fact that there are two types of laws, just and unjust. One has not only a legal but a moral responsibility to obey just laws. One has a moral responsibility to disobey unjust laws. An unjust law is a human law that is not rooted in eternal law and natural law. Any law that uplifts human personality is just, any law that degrades human personality is unjust. An unjust law is a code that a numerical or power majority group compels a minority group to obey but does not make binding on itself." [10]

Some of my readers may be saying, "I thought you were going to stick to religious values, and now you are into politics." Not at all. The two great principles of the Christian religion are love for God and love for humans. The Bible—and especially the Old Testament books of the prophets—are filled with concern for justice and fairness. Since the human race is created in the image of God, we are all brothers and sisters. Whatever defaces or demeans that image attacks the very heart of religion. The Christian may use different methods of righting wrong than the secular politician, but his/her sense of moral outrage is certainly no less.

How Moral Ideas Change

Just because someone can *think* logically does not imply that he will *act* morally. Yet the capacity for logical thinking is necessary in order to advance in moral reasoning, so parents and teachers should work to foster it. Much of Section Three of this book will be devoted to this task, but a few suggestions in closing this chapter will be in order.

Moral ideas change not simply because people teach children "good" moral values but because these children are "challenged in a number of different ways to think more deeply about moral problems." [11] Some of these ways are:

1. Creating moral conflict or disequilibrium (comfortable ideas and beliefs are challenged).

2. Fostering empathy (taking the role of another).

3. Querying how justice is perceived (is the adult fair?).

4. Providing opportunities for democratic dialogue.

Thus the quality of the environment—both at school and at home—influences both the *rate* of moral development and the *stage* eventually reached.

"Children in general have difficulty understanding moral arguments more than one stage higher than their own. Moral positions only one stage above the child's own, in general, create more positive moral conflict and more opportunities for growth than do positions either far above the child's stage of reasoning or below it." [12]

"Arguments at a child's own stage are dismissed as being simple or obvious." [13]

The term *moral conflict* has a negative ring about it, but actually it is absolutely necessary to shake up settled thinking and lead the person to search for more satisfactory explanations to the cosmic questions of life. It goes without saying that wisdom, skill, and love are required of the adult guide in this process.

Notes

[1] Derrick L. Proctor, "Students' Perception of the High School Environment as Related to Moral Development" (Ph.D. diss., Purdue University, 1975).

[2] Kohlberg, "Development of Moral Character," pp. 389, 391.

[3] *Ibid.*, pp. 396-398.

[4] *Ibid.*, p. 400.

[5] *Ibid.*, p. 402.

[6] Hoffman, "Moral Development," pp. 280, 281.

[7] Kohlberg, "Development of Moral Character," p. 408.

[8] *Ibid.*, p. 425

[9] Scharf, McCoy, and Ross, *Growing Up Moral*, p. 11.

[10] In Fraenkel, *How to Teach About Values*, pp. 81, 82.

[11] Scharf et al., *op. cit.*, p. 18.

[12] *Ibid.*, p. 26.

[13] *Ibid.*, p. 19.

CHAPTER 12

Growing Up in Prairie City

Back in the 1940s a team of researchers set up shop in a small Midwestern community designated as "Prairie City." They administered a series of psychological tests to all of the 120 ten-year-old inhabitants. Then they retested the group each year for the next seven years. In addition, they conducted a series of intensive interviews with thirty-four of the young people. The team spent sixteen years studying and writing about the youth of Prairie City and their character development. The report of the findings was written by Robert Peck and fellow researchers, including the famed developmental psychologist Robert Havighurst.[1]

In the previous two chapters we have explored the stages of moral development as presented by Kohlberg. The Prairie City research presents a slightly different, and not as well known, model. Since this longitudinal study is one of the most thorough ever conducted in the field of character development, it deserves our consideration. While still cognitive-developmental, it is also composed of motivational (reasons for acting morally) elements.

This formulation proposes five motivational patterns or character types. The types are actually *components* of character, since no individual is a pure type. One component often predominates, but the person may exhibit other types under different circumstances.

The Five Character Types

The first character type is the *amoral*. The child follows

whims and impulses without regard for how this behavior affects others. Self is the center of the universe, and other people or objects are only a means to self-gratification. The amoral type may be delinquent or "charming but irresponsible"; moral principles, however, have not been internalized. What standards exist consist of a crude, harsh, punitive collection of don'ts. They are repressive, inconsistent, and impossible to follow. The child feels unloved and is incapable of loving. While this stage is normal for the infant in the first year, it may persist into childhood and adolescence. The adult may become psychologically fixated at this level.

The second character type is the *expedient*. The child considers the welfare and reactions of others and conforms to society's definition of moral only to gain personal ends. He/she is not concerned about others except to obtain their approval. This type is more aware than the amoralist of the advantages of conforming to social requirements to gain long-term goals. The expedient youth is not capable of genuine love and interest for others, no matter what counterfeit show may be produced. This pattern is found in young children who have learned to respect the reward-punishment power of adults. External sanctions are always necessary, however, to guide and control behavior. Remove them, and the expedients will relapse into doing whatever they please.

The third pattern is the *conforming* type who operate by one general internalized principle: Do what others do and what they say one "should do"; conform to the rules of the group. These youth experience anxiety for possible disapproval. They learn more by habit than by awareness of moral cause and effect. When they break a rule, they are more likely to suffer shame (fear of disapproval) than guilt (self-condemnation). They define "right" as acting by the rules. If this sometimes hurts others, they feel no guilt, for they have no abstract principles of honesty, loyalty, responsibility, et cetera. They have the capacity to love others and are willing to treat them considerately but have no keen perception of others' needs and feelings. This is the common pattern of middle and late childhood.

The fourth type is the *irrational-conscientious*. These young people judge a given act according to their own internal standards of right and wrong. They conform not to group mores but to an internalized code. They suffer guilt if they fail to live up to their own ideals of what is moral, for they have violated their own integrity.

The type is named *irrational* because of rigidity in the application of the principles. An act is "good" or "bad" because the youth defines it as such, not because of positive or negative effects on others. This pattern is found in children who have accepted and internalized parental rules but have not attained awareness that rules are intended to serve human, functional purposes. They may be so rigidly "moral" that they sometimes act to the detriment of others. Their standards are not accessible to rational investigation and testing but are inflexible, and therefore they are subject to a self-righteous dogmatism. They often feel unloved and unloving but act in conventionally "kind" and "considerate" ways, displaying overt love without essential warmth. This type parallels the conforming type as a stage of character development. It may be considered an alternate method of motivation in later childhood.

The final type is the *rational-altruistic*. This is the highest level, found only (but not usually) in adolescence or adulthood. These people have a stable set of moral principles by which they judge and direct their actions. They assess the results of an act in a given situation and approve it on the ground of whether or not it serves others as well as themselves.

They are *rational* because they assess each new action and its effects in the light of internalized moral principles derived from social experience. They are *altruistic* because they are ultimately as interested in the welfare of others as of themselves and are not interested in pursuing a principle for its own sake, without regard to its human consequences. Their internalized principles are continually open to rational experimentation in order to achieve the moral *purpose* inherent in the principle. They have not compartmentalized their values but have integrated them with their total selves.

These people feel lovable and loved. They are warmly and spontaneously loving, highly perceptive of others' needs and wishes, and give love without making conditions. They are not bargainers. They put themselves in the place of others and do not use them. They see implications beyond the immediate, work constructively, and assume their share of the responsibility. They do what is morally right because they want to. Their public and private values are identical. They are the ideal product of effective values transmission.

Consistency in Character Development

Is moral behavior general—all of one piece—or is it specific to the situation? The Hartshorne and May research had concluded that it was specific and therefore not generalizable across the whole experience. Peck, however, concluded that the question could not be answered so directly—that there are two kinds of consistency.[2]

Inner consistency is internal, the degree of consonance or contradiction among a person's aims and values. It is really a measure of personality integration. Does an internal war rage between acceptable and unacceptable impulses? *Overt conformity* is a measure of the social aspects of character. It is the consistency with which one conforms to the moral code in outward behavior. The latter kind, which was studied by Hartshorne and May, is very likely specific. The former, which is much harder to quantify, may well be general.

Then the range of moral horizon must be considered.[3] Some act morally toward family and friends but consider rivals or strangers "fair game" for exploitation. Others are moral toward those like them in manners, social affiliations, or religion. Some may include citizens of their own nation but exclude "foreigners." Some few, such as Albert Schweitzer, hold every man as brother and act by that belief. To ask if a person is moral in behavior is not sufficient. We must also ask, "Moral toward whom?"

In summary, even though almost everyone has some inconsistencies in daily living, "there does seem to be such a thing as individual character: a persisting pattern of attitudes and motives which produce a rather predictable kind and quality of moral behavior." [4]

Basic character type seems to develop early. "The pattern of motives and typical actions each individual shows by age 10 . . . tends to persist through adolescence." [5] Not that the 10-year-old is capable of the higher stages of moral reasoning, but the youth is likely to stay at the same relative level as his/her peers. For example, those who have the best self-control at 10 will also have the best self-control at 17. Also, the same attitudes and motives in major aspects of morality tend to be maintained. Once allowance is made for normal maturational changes, "it is remarkable how little alteration there is in the basic motive pattern of most adolescents." [6]

Family Influence on Maturity of Character

The Peck model is especially practical because it includes a thorough study of family background on character type. Moral maturity, as measured by the five character components, was found to be strongly related to "consistency of family life" (regularity in the home, consistency of parental control, and common participation in activities) and to "mutual trust and approval among child and parents" (good interparental relations, confidences shared with parents by child, and parental approval of child and his/her activities). [7] It was also moderately related to "democracy versus autocracy of parental control" (sharing in family decisions).

When a character type persists into adolescence, a distinctive family background can be identified. [8] Amoral youth come from families that are markedly inconsistent, highly mistrustful, and disapproving of children. These parents have very little love, little emotional security, and little if any consistent discipline.

Expedient youth are reared in the laissez-faire home where parents give the child indiscriminate freedom, approve of him, and are lenient in discipline but inconsistent in the moral and social patterns set. The child learns to do whatever brings the most gratification. Nothing is asked of him, and he has never learned to make sacrifices.

Conforming youth have parents who are consistent but autocratic, generally employing severe discipline. They may be distrustful and disapproving toward the child (or the opposite), but they are authoritarian, regular in rules and way of life. Irrational-conscientious youth also come from families where consistency of behavior and severity of discipline are found. These homes usually exhibit mild mutual trust, approval, and confidence.

The family background of the rational-altruistic youth is the one of most interest to us in the search for the best ways to transmit values, since this is the character type we would prefer to see developed in our children. In this home we find common participation among the family members, shared confidences, approval of child and peer activities, and harmonious interparental relations. Democratic, regular, consistent control exists. It is not harsh, but not completely lenient, either. The youth confides openly in the parents, and they discuss problems together. The young person is rewarded for the internalization of a consistent moral code and experiences social success in the family. The parents love the child for himself rather than for his desired qualities. "In short, love and discipline are *both* essential, joint determinants of good character." [9]

"The general conclusion seems inescapable that a child's character is the direct product, almost a direct reproduction of the way his parents treat him. As they are to him, so he is to all others." [10]

As to best methods of discipline:

"Lack of discipline, or inconsistent parental control, produced only poor character. Severe, autocratic discipline, consistently applied, produced adolescents who were passively conforming to direction and convention in an unthinking, unautonomous way.

"On the other hand, parental control which was at once consistent, truthful, averse to severe punishment, and giving some limited but growing practice in decision-making—this kind of discipline produced mature, *self-disciplined* adolescents." [11]

We often wonder whether the strong influence of peers will outweigh any good that parents can do in values education. This research concluded that "both character structure and the value content of each adolescent's moral code came predominantly from the family." [12] The early determinants are so powerful that "moral character is shaped predominantly by the family, not *independently* formed or reformed to any great extent by experience in the peer group, in the ordinary case." [13]

"Usually, then, peer forces can be seen acting to reinforce or crystallize behavioral tendencies already present. The peer group is less a causal force than a supporting force in the development of moral character." The same is true with the church, the school, and other people outside the family. [14]

Here, then, is the importance of modeling. This section serves as a bridge between the cognitive-developmental approaches of the past three chapters and the social learning orientation of the coming one. It tells us that young people can be motivated to move through the moral stages by the example of significant people in their lives. Character structures are learned by emulation of those few persons who are emotionally essential to the growing child.

"Moral preaching which is not backed by consonant behavior is largely a waste of time and effort. Indeed, it may often be worse than useless, if it teaches children to say one thing and do another, either through mental confusion or through conscious hypocrisy.

"Children do as we do, not as we say. Their character tends to be an accurate reflection of the way their parents act toward them, no matter what contrary pretenses some parents try to present to society." [15]

How, then, would Peck and his fellow researchers sum up their sixteen-year study?

"The *only* method that works in favor of mature, dependable character is first to give people—whether children or adults—reason to feel an incentive to behave ethically; and then guide them intelligently, patiently, and with growing freedom to make and test their own decisions. . . . *None* of the other methods breeds more than unthinking, rigid compliance at best—and many methods breed savagely hostile revenge behavior." [16]

With this background we turn to the study of how parents and teachers influence learning.

Notes

[1] Robert F. Peck et. al., *The Psychology of Character Development* (New York: John Wiley and Sons, Inc. 1960).

[2] *Ibid.*, pp. 17, 18.

[3] *Ibid.*, pp. 20, 21.

[4] *Ibid.*, p. 164.

[5] *Ibid.*, p. 165.

[6] *Ibid.*

[7] *Ibid.*, p. 106.

[8] *Ibid.*, pp. 109-125.

[9] *Ibid.*, p. 125.

[10] *Ibid.*, p. 178.

[11] *Ibid.*, p. 181.

[12] *Ibid.*, p. 127.

[13] *Ibid.*, p. 129.

[14] *Ibid.*, pp. 150-154.

[15] *Ibid.*, p. 189.

[16] *Ibid.*, p. 192.

CHAPTER 13

Learning Right From Wrong

I really enjoy the porpoise shows at places such as Sea World, Marineland, and other tourist attractions. These aquatic mammals perform amazing feats such as tossing a ball, fetching objects, pulling a raft with people on it, taking bows, and leaping many feet out of the water to snatch a fish from the trainer's mouth.

It's remarkable what animals can be trained to do. Pigeons will play ping-pong, cockatoos ride miniature bicycles, and ducks do a dance. And dogs! Without even mentioning those that perform professionally, I could give quite a description of the abilities of my poodle, Snowflake, starting with "lie down and roll over" and "play dead dog."

Do you know how people teach animals to do these tricks? Trainers use a twofold approach called "shaping" and "reinforcement." As soon as the animal makes a small accidental movement in the direction of the desired behavior, the trainer reinforces it with a morsel of food. The next time it must go just a fraction further in the right direction before being reinforced. The process continues, slowly and patiently, until the animal can perform the trick.

But what about people? Some behavioral scientists, adopting a mechanistic approach, have decided that people are only animals further up the evolutionary ladder and that their behavior is totally dependent upon the shaping power of external forces. John Watson, founder of the psychological school known as behaviorism, said, in essence, "Give me a child young enough, and I can make him into anything I wish." One of the primary laws of learning, set down by pioneer educational psychologist E. L. Thorndike, is that if an action has pleasant consequences, it is likely to be repeated. The idea of a society in which the actions of the citizens are completely determined by outside intervention is portrayed in works such as B. F. Skinner's *Walden II* and Aldous Huxley's *Brave New World*.

The Christian cannot accept this approach, for the Bible affirms that God created humans with free will—the power of choice. The very definition of a value involves choosing and prizing. People are more than robots or trained animals. People cannot abdicate their responsibility for moral judgment and behavior by viewing themselves as helpless chips floating on the wild ocean of their environment.

And yet, the Christian cannot ignore the fact that the way the child develops is strongly influenced by the significant people in his/her life, particularly in the early years. How much does a baby know? Almost nothing. Except for the instinct to suck and a few other very primitive reactions, we have had to learn everything we know as adults. This applies not only to cognitive material but to moral judgment and action—the difference between right and wrong and the desire to choose the right. Therefore, while we will reject the secular, mechanistic applications of behavioral psychology, we will look at social learning theory to discover what it can teach us concerning the way parents and teachers may best help young people learn appropriate Christian values.

Effects of Child-rearing Practices

Martin Hoffman reviewed seventeen research studies in an effort to summarize the relationship between various child-rearing practices and several indices of moral development. He placed the child-rearing practices in four categories:

1. *Power assertion:* The parent uses physical punishment, deprivation of material objects or privileges, force, or

the threat of any of these.

2. *Love withdrawal:* The parent gives direct but non-physical expression to anger or disapproval for some undesirable behavior (ignores child, turns back on child, refuses to speak or listen to child, states a dislike of child, isolates child, or threatens to leave). These practices are more devastating emotionally than power assertion and typically more prolonged.

3. *Induction:* The parent gives reasons for requirements, points out harmful consequences of behavior for self or for others, persuades, appeals to pride or being "grown-up," or explores the implications of behavior for another person.

4. *Affection:* This is not actually a practice but an attitude that pervades practices. The parent provides emotional security and becomes a positive object that the child wishes to please. The child identifies with the parent and adopts his/her attributes.[1]

Hoffman also isolated four indices of moral development from the seventeen research studies:

1. *Resistance to temptation*—the degree to which the individual can be counted on to resist pressures to deviate from a standard even when the possibility of detection and punishment is remote.

2. Amount of *guilt* experienced following failure to comply with a standard.

3. *Internal versus external orientation*—the extent to which moral action is independent of any thoughts about sanctions (disapproval or punishment).

4. The tendency to *confess* and accept responsibility for deviant behavior.[2]

Notice that these indices are generally more behaviorally defined than those of the cognitive-developmentalists, with an overlap on index 3. When the indices of moral development were correlated with the child-rearing practices, some interesting findings appeared.[3]

Power assertion was related to weak moral development to a highly consistent degree, holding true for both sexes and throughout the entire age range of children studied. This was the strongest finding of the review. Love withdrawal had little relation, either positively or negatively, to moral development.

Induction was the practice most conducive to moral development. Some studies showed positive correlations and some showed none, but no studies showed negative correlations. The relationships were not as strong or consistent as the negative ones with power assertion, and the pattern was most clear-cut for guilt and internal moral orientation. Resistance to temptation and confession were more ambiguous. Affection also contributed to moral development, but the evidence in most cases was not as strong as for induction. Induction combined with affection would appear to be the best road to moral maturity.

Identification and Imitation

Since the time of Freud identification has been viewed as the central process in the development of a conscience.[4] The young child becomes motivated to emulate the parent and to internalize those admired characteristics, including moral standards. When those standards are violated, the child experiences guilt. Apart from its psychoanalytic origins, it seems sensible to assume some such process.

Developmental, or *anaclitic*, identification is based on the child's anxiety over possible loss of the parent's love. To reduce this anxiety and assure himself of love, the child strives to become like the parent—to incorporate various parental characteristics. The youth may not identify in all respects, but chooses certain valued parental characteristics. The process is selective rather than total. It is generally easier to identify with moral attributes manifested in overt behavior or communicated verbally than with inner states such as self-criticism and guilt.

As the time drew near for the girls' reception during my senior year at boarding academy, I was not "going steady" with anyone and wondered if I would receive an invitation to this major social event. A note did arrive from a young lady whom I had known for years (we were members of the same local church). Though no "romantic" interest had ever existed between us, we were friends, and the evening might have offered a pleasant occasion. But I knew that my parents, and particularly my mother, had a somewhat unfavorable view of this family because of some things that had happened in the church. Mom also believed this girl to be rather worldly and certainly not a suitable date for her son. I struggled with this decision. It was only a date. And yet Mom would want to know whom I had escorted, and I knew she would be shocked and hurt. So I finally framed a lame excuse and attended the reception at the stag table.

Here is an example of identification related to affection. No power assertion was employed; my parents did not threaten or attempt to force me. Neither was well educated, and they had little knowledge of formal parenting procedures. But they loved me deeply and had great (probably too much) faith in me, and they demonstrated that love and faith in countless ways. Not that I didn't manifest the normal foibles of adolescence and contribute my share to the parental graying process. But I could never deliberately hurt them, and when the chips were down, I couldn't bring myself to disappoint them.

Since young people will identify with their parents, it is important to consider what kinds of attitudes and behaviors we would like to have them imitate. A number of laboratory experiments using models have been carried out in areas such as resistance to temptation, inhibition of aggression, self-denial in performance standards, and deferment of gratification. More evidence has been found "that observation of models is capable of undermining the effects of a child's past socialization in impulse control and self-denial than that it is an effective means of furthering these aspects of moral development." [5] This confirms what we have suspected all along—it is easier to be a bad example than to be a good one.

In spite of this, the weight of research evidence demonstrates that any behavior, including control of aggression and other impulses, can be acquired through imitation and observational learning. As we will continue to see, modeling on the part of parents and teachers is of prime importance in values transmission.

As we look back over the various explanations for how children acquire values, it is apparent that no one theory has a monopoly on the truth. Moral development is complex and multifaceted. Hoffman suggests that moral development proceeds along four tracks whose end products are (1) behavioral conformity, (2) perception of authority as rational, (3) impulse inhibition, and (4) consideration for others.[6] The latter seems particularly appropriate for religious values.

Modeling Values

As Fraenkel reminds us: "Students acquire their values to a large extent through observing and imitating both peer and adult models."[7] In the first section we proposed that religious values have to do with relationships with God and with people. Therefore, parents and teachers need to model the type of behavior that affirms and strengthens these relationships. One of these values is a deep respect for human beings as created in the image of God and therefore important and worthwhile. Fraenkel illustrates how a teacher may use a class discussion to model this value:

1. Accept all statements that students offer, no matter how silly or unusual they may seem when first presented.

2. Do not require students to talk if they do not want to.

3. When a student is having trouble getting his thoughts out, it is helpful sometimes to restate what he has expressed without indicating approval or disapproval of his ideas.

4. Tell students that you want them to offer their ideas.

5. Take care not to impose your views on students.

6. Don't hesitate to introduce ideas contrary to those expressed by students in order to bring out other aspects of an issue.[8]

Are these *religious* values? It depends. For some they

may reflect merely the perspective of humanism. But for many of us, our view of the dignity and worthwhileness of people is derived from the Word of God. God created man and woman in His own image and esteemed them of such value that He sent His beloved Son to die for them. Therefore, our relationships with people are genuinely religious. The Bible is emphatic that religion has a horizontal as well as a vertical dimension. Since our relationship to God is private and internal, most of our modeling will necessarily be done on the horizontal plane. "All men will know that you are my disciples if you love one another" (John 13:35).

"Values do not come merely by imitation. It may be, however, that the availability of a model makes it easier for a child to comprehend what a value is actually like in practice, and thus makes it more likely that that value would be chosen, thoughtfully and freely, than would be if the model were not available for observation." [9]

I like to think of value transmission as a huge smorgasbord where all the tempting dishes of competing values are displayed. Here the youth will eventually get to choose the items that are most appealing to them. And which will they choose? Those that are most colorful and attractive, most delectable, most tasty! It is not our responsibility to force our values upon our young people. It is our responsibility to model our values so attractively that these youth cannot help seeing that they are vastly superior to the competition, and will freely choose them.

Ellen White counsels: "Parents must see that their own hearts and lives are controlled by the divine precepts, if they would bring up their children in the nurture and admonition of the Lord. They are not authorized to fret and scold and ridicule. They should never taunt their children with perverse traits of character, which they themselves have transmitted to them." [10]

John Gardner summed it up nicely when he stated that young people "do not learn ethical principles; they emulate ethical (or unethical) people. They do not analyze or list the attributes they wish to develop; they identify with people who seem to have these attributes. That is why young people need models." [11]

Notes

[1] Hoffman, "Moral Development," pp. 285, 286.

[2] *Ibid.*, pp. 286-290.

[3] *Ibid.*, p. 292.

[4] *Ibid.*, pp. 305, 306.

[5] *Ibid.*, p. 316.

[6] *Ibid.*, p. 345.

[7] Fraenkel, *How to Teach About Values*, p. 137.

[8] *Ibid.*, pp. 138-141.

[9] Raths et al., *Values and Teaching*, p. 226.

[10] Ellen G. White, *Fundamentals of Christian Education* (Nashville: Southern Pub. Assn., 1923), p. 67.

[11] Gardner, *Self-renewal*, p. 124.

CHAPTER 14

A Chip Off the Old Block

In a recent interesting study on values transmission, Hart Nelsen surveyed 2,774 young people in the fourth through the eighth grades.[1] He determined the religiosity of these preadolescents by five measures: (1) frequency of prayer, (2) reading the Bible, (3) attending religious services, (4) belief in the Ten Commandments, and (5) belief in biblical literalism. To measure parental religiosity, he asked the students how often their parents attend church and the amount of interest that the parents have in religion. Similarly, asking the youth how often the parents argue and fight with each other created an index of family discord.

Parental religiosity significantly predicted the religiosity of the youth. Those parents who attended church more frequently and who communicated the impression that religion was important in their lives tended to have children with strong religious values. On discord, the results were mixed. Religiosity was highest in the youth where parents were religious *and* in harmony. It was lowest where parents were not religious but in harmony. Discord especially affected boys negatively. Thus, harmony between the parents is an important factor in values transmission, but only when that harmony is built around the vital place of religious values in the parents' own lives.

In previous chapters in this section we have examined the major theories as to how moral development occurs. In this connection we have noted some of the significant pioneering research that has undergirded those theories. In this chapter we turn to a brief review of more recent research on values transmission between parent and child.

Value Differences Between Generations

Many studies have shown that youth are likely to be less conservative than their parents. This is part of the adolescent process of growing up—of cutting the apron strings and reaching out to find a separate identity from the parents. A few examples:

Sam Payne and associates investigated values differences across three generations.[2] College students, parents, and grandparents completed an eighty-five-item questionnaire indicating how bad they would feel if they engaged in the described behaviors. The students were least severe in their judgments, then the parents, followed by the grandparents. Cross-section studies of this type, of course, cannot determine whether these differences are enduring or whether they reveal areas of concern that emerge at specific points as the individuals pass through the various stages of life. It is certainly possible that the youth will become nearly as conservative as their parents when they reach the same age.

A study of the relative influence of mothers and fathers on religious socialization among 653 parent-youth triads found that the group means on value items were clearly different despite a high degree of within-family predictivity.[3] An interesting sidelight is that the young people tended to perceive the parents as much more traditional and conservative than the parents see themselves. Adolescents have a need to place value distance between themselves and adult authority figures as part of the process of forming a separate identity.

Benjamin Keeley surveyed students at a Midwestern university and their parents to discover if there were intergenerational differences in religious beliefs and behaviors. The data revealed significant differences on most items. The adults were more traditional, more conforming, and more structured. The youth were more spontaneous and more open to change and newness.[4]

Stephen Wieting conducted a comparison of sixty-six family units of Protestants on both religious belief and religious activity. Adolescents were significantly lower than their parents on religious activity dimensions such as attendance at church, communal involvement, friends in the local parish, and choice of church over other activities. The difference was not as clear-cut on the belief dimensions. While the youth were significantly lower than their parents on the importance of religion, no difference was found on belief in omnipotent control or on religion being private rather than communal.[5]

Value Similarities Between Generations

Now before you decide that the younger generation is "going to the dogs," you should know that much research has found that children tend to resemble their parents in attitudes and behaviors. Even though the youth may be less traditional, they are still likely to follow along a similar pathway. This is both encouraging and frightening, for it lays a huge responsibility on parental shoulders. Some examples:

In a study of one hundred college students and their parents, Troll and associates concluded that members of a family do resemble each other in values and to a lesser extent in personality traits. They further stated that "individuals from the same family tend to be more like each other than like unrelated people." [6]

A three-generation study of eighty-eight families indicated that the family is powerful compared to other agencies in transmitting religious identity as defined by church affiliation. The ones who conducted it declared the family to be the crucial agency of socialization, even though the transmission of norms is not equal for all values. The greatest continuity was in the all-female lineage. The authors conclude that the keepers of religious heritage in the United States are women.[7] Incidentally, the research on the relative influence of mothers and fathers on values transmission has been mixed. The influence of mothers has been found stronger in some studies and on some items, while others have favored the fathers.

Richard Kalish and Ann Johnson conducted a three-generation study, consisting of fifty-three young women, their mothers, and their grandmothers. The highest similarities existed between mother and daughter generations—even higher than for mother and grandmother. The authors speculated that this could be a result of the amount of intimate contact between the mothers and their daughters.[8]

William McCready investigated the process of religious socialization—in this case, the passing of patterns of devotional behavior from one generation to another—in a national sample of American Catholics. He found that an intergenerational transmission of devotional behavior does exist, and the father is the dominant source of influence. In addition, parental influence outweighs any social class effect.[9]

So abundant evidence exists that parents influence to at least some extent the process of values formation in their offspring. The big question is What parental attitudes and practices are most likely to facilitate the acquiring of intrinsic religious values? Recent research is also helpful here.

Factors Contributing to Values Transmission

Glen Elder explored three styles of parental government (autocratic, democratic, and permissive) and their effect on the adolescent. He found that adolescents were more likely to follow parental models who explained rules frequently when asked to do so. Furthermore, democratic parents were more attractive as models, regardless of the frequency of their explanations.[10]

Martin Johnson investigated the relationship between the religious commitment of students and their perceptions of their parents' religiosity, family warmth, and acceptance. He found that religious commitment was related to a warm, supportive family and highly correlated with religious influences in the home. He concluded that students report their parents as generally similar to themselves in religious commitment and that religious students tend to perceive their families as warmer, happier, and more accepting than do nonreligious students.[11]

Snell Putney and Russell Middleton studied the religious convictions of 1,088 college students. Their strongest finding was that young people are most likely to accept a religious ideology if it is held jointly by both parents. If the parents were not in agreement, the students inclined toward the parent closest to the modernist Christian position or toward the position of the mother.[12]

Parent behaviors as determinants of adolescent religiosity among Catholic high school students is the subject of a most helpful book-length research report. The authors constructed two dimensions of parental behavior. *Support* is the quality of interaction that is perceived by youth as the parents establishing a positive, affective relationship (helps in problems, says nice things, makes me feel he is there if I need him). *Control* is the quality perceived by youth as constraining them to do what the parents want (strict about what is expected, pushes me to do my best, keeps after me to do things).[13]

The researchers also defined four dimensions of religiosity: (1) belief (God, divinity of Christ, miracles, devil), (2) practice (church attendance, communion, confession, prayer), (3) experience (presence of God, communication from God, salvation, temptation), and (4) knowledge (biblical and church history). These findings emerged:

1. Adolescents who perceived a high degree of support *and* control from either the mother or father or from both parents showed significantly greater commitment to traditional religiosity.

2. Support from mother and father had greater influence than control by them in determining youth attitudes and behaviors.

3. Adolescents who experienced low support and high

control were most often associated with the lowest degree of religiosity.

4. These findings applied to the dimensions of belief, practice, and experience, but not to knowledge.[14]

Dean Hoge and associates researched religious values transmission with 254 triads (father, mother, tenth-graders) from Catholic, Southern Baptist, and Methodist churches. They found the denomination to be more powerful than the family in predicting youth values. However, transmission across the generations was strongest when (1) the parents were younger, (2) the parents agreed on definite religious beliefs, (3) the values were visible, concrete, and of lasting concern to the parents, rather than abstract or transient, (4) the parents actively carried out religious socialization in the home, and (5) the overall disagreements between parent and child were small.[15]

From the research we have surveyed we might summarize the factors that are most conducive to the transmission of parental values:

1. Parents themselves have strong religious values.

2. Parents agree with each other on the content of those values.

3. Parents live in harmony with their stated values.

4. Parents get along well with each other. They do not often argue and fight but live in an atmosphere of marital harmony.

5. Parents operate a democratic family government, allowing input from the children and being willing to explain the reasons for necessary rules.

6. Parents are warm and loving toward their children and accepting of them.

7. Parents mingle firm control with high support. Discipline is love-oriented.

8. Parents and children get along well together, rarely arguing and fighting.

9. Parents actively teach their religious principles to their children.

This last finding from contemporary research reflects the counsel given long ago by God to His people: "These commandments that I give you today are to be upon your hearts. Impress them on your children. Talk about them when you sit at home and when you walk along the road, when you lie down and when you get up" (Deut. 6:6, 7). However, all evidence indicates that teaching that is not backed up by loving, joyous practice is not only worthless but may produce rebellion or encourage hypocrisy.

Ellen White writes that teachers (and parents are teachers) should step down from their high position and say to the young people: "Let us climb together, and we will see what can be gained by a united study of the Scriptures. . . . Let us study together. . . . If any explanation of the word differs from your previous understanding, do not hesitate to state your views of the subject. Light will shine upon us as in the meekness and lowliness of Christ we study together." [16]

Notes

[1] Hart M. Nelson, "Gender Differences in the Effects of Parental Discord on Preadolescent Religiousness," *Journal for the Scientific Study of Religion* 20 (December, 1981): 351-360.

[2] Sam Payne, David A. Summers, and Thomas R. Stewart, "Value Differences Across Three Generations," *Sociometry* 36 (March, 1973): 20-30.

[3] Alan C. Acock and Vern L. Bengtson, "On the Relative Influence of Mothers and Fathers: A Covariance Analysis of Political and Religious Socialization," *Journal of Marriage and the Family* 40 (August, 1978): 519-530.

[4] Benjamin J. Keeley, "Generations in Tension: Intergenerational Differences and Continuities in Religion and Religion-related Behavior," *Review of Religious Research* 17 (Spring, 1976): 21-31.

[5] Stephen G. Wieting, "An Examination of Intergenerational Patterns of Religious Belief and Practice," *Sociological Analysis* 36 (Summer, 1975): 137-149.

[6] Lillian E. Troll, Bernice L. Neugarten, and Ruth J. Kraines, "Similarities in Values and Other Personality Characteristics in College Students and Their Parents," *Merrill-Palmer Quarterly* 15 (October, 1969): 323-336.

[7] Joan Aldous and Reuben Hill, "Social Cohesion, Lineage Type, and Intergenerational Transmission," *Social Forces* 43 (May, 1965): 471-482.

[8] Richard Kalish and Ann Johnson, "Value Similarities and Differences in Three Generations of Women," *Journal of Marriage and the Family* 34 (February 1972): 49-54.

[9] William C. McCready, "Faith of Our Fathers: A Study of the Process of Religious Socialization," (Ph.D. diss., University of Illinois at Chicago Circle, 1972).

[10] Glen H. Elder, Jr., "Parental Power Legitimation and Its Effect on the Adolescent," *Sociometry* 26 (March, 1963): 50-65.

[11] Martin A. Johnson, "Family Life and Religious Commitment," *Review of Religious Research* 14 (Spring, 1973): 144-150.

[12] Snell Putney and Russell Middleton, "Rebellion, Conformity, and Parental Religion

Ideologies," *Sociometry* 24 (June, 1961): 125-135.

[13] Darwin L. Thomas, Viktor Gecas, Andrew Weigert, and Elizabeth Rooney, *Family Socialization and the Adolescent* (Lexington, Mass.: D.C. Heath, 1974).

[14] *Ibid.*, pp. 87-110.

[15] Dean R. Hoge, et al., "Adolescent Religious Socialization: A Study of Goal Priorities According to Parents and Religious Educators," *Review of Religious Research* 23 (March, 1982): 226-304; Dean R. Hoge, Gregory H. Petrillo, and Ella I. Smith, "Transmission of Religious and Social Values from Parents to Teenage Children," *Journal of Marriage and the Family* 44 (August, 1982): 569-580.

[16] Ellen G. White, *Counsels to Parents and Teachers* (Mountain View, Calif.: Pacific Press Pub. Assn., 1943), p. 436.

CHAPTER 15

But What About Seventh-day Adventists?

Studies of religious value transmission, while valuable, pose a problem for Adventists and other conservative denominations. The problem is that value statements are often given in such general terms that nearly every member of these churches would agree with them. For example, surveys often ask respondents about their beliefs in God, the literal truth of the Bible, the divinity of Christ, and the reality of life after death. While people from various religious persuasions might well divide on these questions, it is doubtful that Adventists would reject any of these. And where there is no difference, there is nothing to study.

Therefore, I decided to do original research on a national sample of Adventist families. For this project my wife, Margaret G. (Peggy) Dudley, a doctoral student in counseling and human services at Andrews University, joined me.

We employed the same general method of Hoge, with two major changes. First, we constructed a more specific measure of values. We wished to include items about which Adventists might differ, depending upon their position on a traditional to nontraditional continuum. Second, by choosing subjects who were all from one religious faith, we averted the problem of having denominational differences overpower the parental effect, as it did in the Hoge study.

On the basis of previous research, we hypothesized that Adventist adolescents as a group are less traditional than their parents in their value attitudes. On the other hand, we proposed that individual young people still resemble their parents to some extent—more traditional parents will tend to have more traditional children and less traditional parents, less traditional children—even though a gap remains between them. We believed that these relationships would hold true both for individual value attitudes and for an overall scale created from the attitudes.

Research Instrument

We developed and piloted a questionnaire that we labled the Intergenerational Value Survey (IVS). In its final form the IVS contained twenty-two statements that deal with the beliefs and behaviors of Seventh-day Adventists. A person could respond to each statement by choosing one of five positions, ranging from "strongly disagree" through "strongly agree." We then assigned scores of 1 through 5 for each choice, with negatively worded statements being scored 5 through 1. In addition to the value statements, we asked for four items of personal information: (1) whether or not a baptized Adventist, (2) highest grade of education reached, (3) years spent in Adventist schools, and (4) sex. The complete wording of the twenty-two value statements is as follows:

WORDING OF ITEMS ON
INTERGENERATIONAL VALUE SURVEY

1. The Bible is relevant to today's problems, and I use its principles in making decisions.
2. The Seventh-day Adventist Church is God's true remnant church.
3. Ellen White was inspired by God, and her writings are an authoritative guide for Christians today.
4. The church has an important place in my life.
5. I believe that God hears and answers my prayers.
6. A Christian should give tithe and offerings before spending any of his or her income on other things.
7. People of various races should worship together

freely and with equality.

8. In the choice of a life profession the most important factor is being of service to others.

9. Any position that a man holds should be open to a qualified woman.

10. There is no place for alcohol or tobacco in the full and happy life.

11. Recreational drugs such as marijuana should be legalized.

12. Vegetarianism is preferable as a lifestyle to meat eating.

13. The Sabbath should be reserved for devotional and witnessing activities and not be made a day of general recreation.

14. It is all right to attend the movies if the pictures are carefully selected.

15. Homosexual behavior is a sin.

16. It is wrong to engage in premarital petting.

17. Premarital sexual intercourse is not wrong if two people really love each other.

18. Abortion is never an option for terminating a pregnancy.

19. Divorce is a valid option when marriage is unhappy.

20. A Christian should be willing to serve in the military as long as such service does not conflict with God's commands.

21. Under some circumstances a Christian could be justified in killing another person.

22. Christians should not wear decorative jewelry.

We also totaled the scores for twenty of the items (all but 7 and 9) to give an overall measure of value attitudes. We labled this the Value Attitude Scale (VAS). We omitted the two items from the scale because a computer analysis revealed they did not correlate well with the rest of the statements, but we left them in the questionnaire because of our interest in their content.

Methods

From a list of Adventist churches in the United States with a membership of more than five hundred, we randomly selected twenty. We asked the pastor of each church or his appointee to serve as a liaison who would give a packet to twenty high school-age youth in the congregation. We chose larger churches in the hopes of finding at least twenty potential subjects.

The packets contained three envelopes—each with a copy of the IVS clearly marked respectively as youth, mother, or father. Each filled out his or her survey privately and sealed it back in the individual envelope. Then the youth sealed the three envelopes in the larger packet and returned it to the liaison,who returned it to us. Since the liaison saw only sealed packets and we did not know who the people were, this procedure guaranteed confidentiality.

Collection of the data was a lengthy process, occupying about six months and involving a series of follow-up letters and phone calls. Eventually we received usable surveys from 712 individuals in 247 families located in every region of the country. Of these families, 218 were complete triads (youth, father, mother), 26 were youth-mother dyads, and 3 were youth-father dyads.

Findings

We did indeed find a difference between the generations. The average VAS score for the youth was significantly different from the average VAS for the mothers and the fathers. Significant differences also existed between youth and fathers on twelve of the twenty-two individual items and between youth and mothers on nineteen of the items. In all comparisons the youth were less traditional than the parents.

But we also found similarities. The youth VAS was significantly correlated with both the mothers' and the fathers' VAS. Significant correlations existed between the youth and the fathers on fifteen of the twenty-two individual items and between youth and mothers on sixteen of the items. All correlations were in the positive direction. In addition, we were able to construct a prediction equation in which three items contributed significantly to the prediction of a young person's Value Attitude Scale. The three, in their order of strength, were (1) mother VAS, (2) father VAS, and (3) whether or not youth had been baptized (those who had were more traditional).

I have omitted many of the technical details of this study that may not be of interest to the general reader and that are available elsewhere.[1] The conclusions, however, are very pertinent to our search together. They may be summarized as follows:

1. The findings of this research generally support the hypotheses. This is in harmony with previous scholarly investigation and assures us that values transmission among Adventists follows much the same pattern as it does in other families.

2. A generation gap concerning values exists, with adolescents *as a group* less traditional than their parents. As a group, mothers are the most traditional, followed by the fathers, and then by the youth. Of course, individual families may differ from this pattern.

3. In spite of this gap, youth tend to resemble their parents in religious values held. While the youth lean toward the nontraditional end of the scale, they tend to vary with their parents on the traditional to nontraditional continuum. Thus, more traditional parents tend to have children who are more traditional than their peers, although less traditional than their parents. And less traditional parents tend to have children who are less traditional than their peers and also even less traditional than their parents.

4. The values of mothers are greater predictors of the values of youth than are the values of fathers. Even though a greater difference exists between youth and mothers as groups than between youth and fathers, individual youth

are somewhat more likely to vary on the traditional continuum with the mother than they are with the father. This supports the literature that suggests that mothers have greater influence on the value development of children than do fathers.

This last conclusion is also in harmony with Ellen White's affirmation that "Next to God, the mother's power for good is the strongest known on earth. . . . The child is more readily impressed by the life and example of the mother than by that of the father, for a stronger and more tender bond of union unites them." [2]

Exhibit R—Romania

The country of Romania provides one of the most amazing success stories for Seventh-day Adventism. Generally speaking, Adventists have not had the growth in European countries that they have experienced in other areas of the world. Romania, with more than fifty thousand members, is a shining exception. A report from Alf Lohne states that the greatest problem that the movement faces is to provide seating for all the members and visitors who crowd into the houses of worship every Sabbath.

The explanation for the rapid spread of the Advent message in Romania, especially in comparison with its only moderate progress in neighboring countries, is complex and cannot be attributed to a single cause. Nevertheless, the influence of parents is worth considering, as suggested in this excerpt from Lohne's report:

"I was told that 70 percent of the church members are young people. After visiting several churches and speaking to several large meetings, I have no doubt that this is true. I also learned that 80 percent of the children in Adventist families join the church. How can this be explained in a country where not only do we not have any church schools or church-operated educational institutions of any kind but also no youth paper or special books for children and youth?

"The explanation I received was that the parents lead

their children and young people to Christ. Parents demonstrate to their children that the values they have found in the church are greater than those offered anywhere else [the whole point of chapter 13]. The church also plays an important role in winning young people to Christ. It involves the youth in activities that go on in the churches most of the day on Sabbaths. In most churches, at least one Sabbath a month the afternoon program is a family hour, in which topics of interest to the whole family are presented. These meetings are open to the public, and many visitors attend." [3]

I would not suggest that Romanian methods will work as well in all places. However, abundant evidence supports the statement "Parents demonstrate to their children that the values they have found in the church are greater than those offered anywhere else" as a universal principle. It is the very foundation of values transmission. "In the formation of character, no other influences count so much as the influence of the home. The teacher's work should supplement that of the parents, but is not to take its place. [4]

Notes

[1] Margaret Dudley, "A Study of the Transmission of Religious Values From Parents to Adolescents" (project report, Andrews University, 1984).

[2] Ellen G. White, *The Adventist Home* (Nashville: Southern Pub. Assn., 1952), p. 240.

[3] Alf Lohne, "Adventist Crowds Create Unique Problems in Romania," *Adventist Review*, Feb. 9, 1984, pp. 14, 15.

[4] White, *Education*, p 283.

How to Teach Values

CHAPTER 16

Using Moral Dilemmas

Betsy had been dating Howard for several months. She was very much in love, and Howard told her that he loved her too. They were both 16 and in high school, but they talked about getting married someday when they had finished their education and Howard had a good job. Then Betsy discovered that she was pregnant. Almost in a panic, she told Howard. He seemed very uneasy and finally said, "I'll marry you now if you insist. But you know I don't have a job, and I have to finish school to get a decent one. Why don't you have an abortion? I've heard of someone who would help arrange it. You can go in and come back out the same day. Neither of us would have to leave school, and no one would be the wiser. Besides, it's not a real person in there yet. Just some tissue. Like taking your tonsils out, only easier."

Betsy had some real qualms about an abortion. She confided in a friend who told her that she knew a place a girl could go and stay until after the baby had come, and then the home would arrange for the baby to be adopted. That way no one would know her secret—but, of course, she would have to drop out of school. She finally got up enough courage to tell her parents. They were very understanding and said that if she wanted to stay home and have the baby, they would help her raise it. She could continue at school, even though she would have to live down some embarrassment and shame. Betsy and her parents are members of a conservative Christian church.

What should Betsy do? Should she (1) marry Howard

immediately, (2) have an abortion, (3) give the baby up for adoption, (4) keep and raise the baby with her parents' help, or (5) choose some other option? What are your reasons for your choice? How do Betsy's religious values influence her decision?

The above story is an example of a moral dilemma. In this final section of the book I will describe and illustrate a number of methods for parents and teachers to use in encouraging the development of values in young people. This is the how-to section. In this chapter I will concentrate on the moral dilemma. Subsequent chapters will deal with other strategies.

The What and Why of Dilemmas

The strategy of using moral dilemmas grows out of cognitive-developmental theory and especially the six moral stages of Kohlberg described in chapters 10 and 11. A moral dilemma is "a conflict situation in which what's right or wrong isn't clear-cut or obvious." [1] Effective dilemmas:

1. Present conflicting claims, both or all of which on the surface appear to be reasonable.

2. Involve some life experience that's real to the participants' own situations.

3. Focus primarily on the *ethical* issues in the case (for us this means those issues decided by religious principles).

4. Open the way for discussion questions that force youth to think more deeply about the moral issues (that is, at a higher stage of moral reasoning). [2]

Why use moral dilemmas? Peter Scharf answers: "As students in a group respond to a dilemma, they naturally offer different concepts of what they believe to be right and wrong. The sharing of diverse moral opinions forces students in the group to either clarify and reiterate their own moral stances or to integrate the opinions of others into their own moral beliefs. This sharing of moral reasoning also forces each of the participants to experience conflict, or disequilibrium, as he or she finds his or her ideas challenged by the ideas and viewpoints of others.

This atmosphere of conflict is an ideal environment for moral growth, for the more a child is exposed to thinking at a stage higher than his or her own, the more likely the child will be to move to that stage." [3]

Kohlberg and Wasserman set forth the following conditions for conducting successful moral dilemmas:

1. Exposure to the next higher stage of reasoning.

2. Exposure to situations posing problems and contradictions for the child's current moral structure (not the content, but the way of thinking), leading to dissatisfaction with his/her current level.

3. An atmosphere of interchange and dialogue where conflicting views can be compared in an open manner.

4. Opportunities afforded for role taking (seeing things from the viewpoint of others).

5. A high level of justice within the environment or institution. [4]

It is obvious that this strategy is primarily tailored to a group setting where the discussion can include reasoning from various stages. However, it can be adapted to a home situation where parent is one-to-one with child. Here the parent must carefully probe and tactfully challenge the thinking of the youth.

How to Conduct a Dilemma Discussion

Fraenkel shares some helpful guidelines for conducting the moral dilemma discussion. [5] I have summarized them and added some comments:

1. Present the dilemma in written, oral, or visual form.

2. Get students to take a tentative position with reasons why. One way to accomplish this is to have them write down what they think the character should do and the reasons for their position *before* they are influenced by other opinions during the discussion.

3. Now have them state their positions and discuss the reasoning behind them.

4. If insufficient disagreement is aroused, complicate the dilemma by adding other factors using "What if?"

questions. For example, in our opening dilemma: What if Howard refused to marry Betsy? What if abortions were illegal in their state? What if her parents were so rigid that Betsy felt she couldn't let them find out that she was pregnant? What if Betsy and Howard attended a Christian school of high standards and would both have been expelled if the school authorities discovered what had happened? What if the pregnancy had been the result of a rape? Would any of these situations change the moral and religious values involved? If so, how? and why?

5. Use probe questions during the discussion.
   a. Clarifying probe: What do you mean by immoral?
   b. Issue-specific probe: What obligations do you owe to a friend?
   c. Inter-issue probe: Which is more important, loyalty to a friend or obligation to obey the law?
   d. Role-switch probe: From the point of view of the parents, should Betsy go to the abortion clinic?
   e. Universal-consequences probe: Is it ever right to have an abortion?

6. Have students summarize reasons for each possible choice. Then have them make a personal choice and write down why they decided it was the best. Don't call for a public declaration (or vote), since doing so might imply that there is one correct answer—a conclusion antithetical to this strategy.

The free sharing of opinions with a Socratic probing and challenging of them characterize dilemma discussions. Scharf adds these suggestions:

1. Clarify the facts within the dilemma.
2. Clarify the ethical (religious) issues.
3. Create an atmosphere of trust by showing respect for each contribution. Challenge the reasoning but never the integrity or worth of the young person.
4. Explore as many options as possible.
5. Deliberately place various opinions in conflict with each other.
6. Resolve inadequacies in arguments. However, not

everyone has to agree on one solution.[6]

As to moving the reasoning up the moral ladder:

"Try to pose a higher stage contradiction to [an] argument. But do this cautiously. Think of a situation for which their argument wouldn't work, or come up with a conflicting moral force which runs counter to that argument (your friend, your parent, the law). The object, of course, is to force the students to confront the inadequacy of their argument." [7]

The use of moral dilemmas calls for careful timing. "The exact moment at which a behavioral problem is occurring is not the best time to begin a moral discussion about it." [8] A better time to introduce an appropriate dilemma is after the emotions have calmed down and the problem can be viewed more objectively.

A Few Examples

But where do I find suitable moral dilemmas? Keep your eyes open, and you'll begin to discover them in such places as books, church papers, newsmagazines, current happenings. Here are three that I picked up in a workshop by Kenneth Blanton:

The Phone Call

School vacation is over, and the young people are returning to boarding school. The weather becomes bad, and the family is concerned about their children arriving safely at school. The parents ask the children that upon arrival at school they are to call back home person-to-person and ask for themselves. The parents will tell the operator that the ones asked for are not there, but they will know the youth have arrived safely. In this way they will not have to pay for a telephone call.

What should the young people do? Why? No phone company rules have been violated, since the person-to-person call was not completed. So does a moral issue even exist? Is it more important to honor your parents or the phone company?

Sabbath Afternoon

While camping with several other Adventist families, one family suggests on Sabbath afternoon that they all take a boatride up the lake to a waterfall.

Would this be acceptable to you? What if, once at the waterfall, some wanted to jump in and swim around a bit? What if someone wanted to be towed on water skis behind the boat? Suppose they have no powerboat but would like to go by canoe to the waterfall? What religious reasons would you give for your answers?

CB Sam

Sam has a very fine high-powered auto and is frustrated by the fifty-five-mile-per-hour speed limit. He frequently uses his CB radio unit to obtain information on the police situation on the stretch of highway ahead of him. He lowers his speed if he learns that someone has spotted a patrol car.

Is this morally right? Why? Would it make a difference if he were using a radar detector, illegal in his state, rather than a CB? Why should (or shouldn't) a Christian obey traffic laws? Or does this subject have anything to do with religion? If a minister preaches at two services on Sabbath morning and has to exceed the legal speed limit to get to the second church on time, is that more justifiable than Sam's speeding on a pleasure jaunt?

With a little practice you can write your own dilemmas. Identify a moral area in which you wish to stimulate thinking, sketch out a simple story, and construct some probe questions. Let's try one:

The Initiation

At last, Wayne is beginning his senior year at boarding academy. The first evening several of his friends come excitedly into his dorm room. Ralph speaks for the group: "Tonight we've got to initiate these new freshmen. They need to know that the seniors are in charge around here. We are going to round them up and throw them in the shower with their clothes on. The dean's out of the building right now. Come on!"

"But that wouldn't be a very friendly welcome to academy life," Wayne protests.

"Oh, come on. A little water's not going to hurt anybody," Ralph urges. "It's all in fun."

Should Wayne (1) join in the initiation, (2) decline and stay in his room, (3) reason with the fellows, (4) stand up for the freshmen even if he too gets thrown in the shower, (5) tell the dean, or (6) choose some other option? Why? What religious values are involved here? If the hazing consisted of more dangerous practices such as tying the newcomers in the woods overnight, would that make a difference? Why might a student wish to participate in a hazing?

Space prohibits us from developing any more dilemmas in detail, but let's scan a list of suggestions:

1. A bully terrorizes a boy. Then the bully has an accident, is pinned under debris, and pleads for help.

2. Mary observes Vanessa cheating. Vanessa gets the class award. Should Mary report the cheating?

3. Bert befriends a loner, and the other students withdraw from Bert, too. He is told he can keep his popularity only by dropping his new friend.

4. Phil sees a friend shoplift a cheap item. What should he do? Would it make a difference if the item were expensive?

5. Jill is asked for a date by a fellow of another race. How should she handle it? What if she knew her parents would be very opposed to the date?

6. Clarence's parents promise him he can go on a trip with the class if he cleans the garage. He does—and they change their mind. Should he "get even"?

7. Tammy knows that her brother is taking drugs, but he made her promise she wouldn't tell. Her parents ask her why he has been acting so different lately.

8. Rosa Parks, a black woman, wouldn't give up her bus seat to a white man as required by the law. She thus started the Montgomery bus boycott. Was she morally

justified?

9. Brother Andrew broke the laws of several Communist countries by smuggling Bibles into them so that their citizens could have access to the Word of God. Was this right? If the border guard asked him what he was carrying, would it be right to lie or at least to evade the question?

10. Throughout its history an Adventist congregation has had only males serve in the top leadership position of elder. Now the church is to vote whether or not women can serve in this capacity. Some say that Scripture tells women to keep quiet in church and to be submissive to their husbands. Others believe that all people are created in the image of God and no discrimination should be made in church service on the basis of external characteristics. How would you vote? Why? What religious values are at stake here?

11. A neighbor is cruel to his animals. Would it be right to let his dog loose when he isn't looking? Report him to the SPCA? What about medical research experiments that use animals? Seal hunts? Other hunting? What should a Christian do?

12. What about a blood transfusion or chemotherapy for a child if the practice is against the religion of the parents? Would it make a difference if the child wants the treatment? If the child doesn't? Is religion or human life the higher value if they conflict?

We could go on and on, but space forces me to stop. The possibilities are limitless. Try out a few on the youth for whom you are responsible. They are guaranteed to stimulate the moral faculties of the brain.

Notes

[1] Scharf et. al., *Growing Up Moral,* p. 31.

[2] *Ibid.,* p. 32.

[3] *Ibid.,* p. 31.

[4] Kohlberg and Wasserman, "The Cognitive-Developmental Approach," p. 563.

[5] Fraenkel, *How to Teach About Values,* pp. 61-67.

[6] Scharf et al., *op. cit.,* pp. 33-40.

[7] *Ibid.,* p. 65.

[8] *Ibid.,* p. 44.

CHAPTER 17

Values Clarification

Amy is leaving church school at the end of the day. She pauses for a moment by her teacher's desk and shares a bit of information. "Mrs. Green, tonight is my favorite TV program, Mayhem." Consider how Mrs. Green might respond.

1. "Umm, that's nice." 2. "Amy, you shouldn't watch all that violence." 3. "Would you rather watch the program than do almost anything else?" The first response is approving or at least noncommittal, and the second is judgmental. Only the third "puts the ball back in the child's court" and calls for Amy, in some small way, to consider her values.

This is the strategy of values clarification. In chapter 8 we described the seven criteria of a value, organized under the three headings of choosing, prizing, and acting. Values clarification techniques are based on this model. The best way to help children develop values, according to Louis Raths and his associates, is to facilitate each of the seven criteria. In other words:

1. Encourage them to make choices and make them freely.

2. Help them discover and examine alternatives when faced with choices.

3. Help them weigh alternatives, reflecting on the consequences of each choice.

4. Encourage them to consider what they cherish.

5. Give them opportunities to make public affirmations of their choices.

6. Encourage them to act in accordance with their choices.

7. Help them to examine repeated behavior patterns in their lives.[1]

Socrates once said, "The unexamined life is not worth living." Clarifying questions start thought processes in motion that lead to deeper reflection and ultimately to action. While these questions do not pass judgment on the response, according to Barbara Glaser and Howard Kirschenbaum, they are not value-free. They are based on the assumption "that thoughtfully reflecting on one's values and life choices is better than not doing so; that it is better to consider alternatives and their consequences than not to; that it is important to act in ways that are consistent with one's value positions; and that it is better to be aware of one's feelings and behavior patterns than to be oblivious or to deny one's inner experience.[2]

The Clarifying Response

While the values clarification method uses a number of techniques, the clarifying response is at the heart of the approach. Most of the other techniques are modifications and extensions of this foundational strategy. Clarifying responses are used "to raise questions in the mind of the student, to prod him gently to examine his life, his actions, and his ideas, with the expectation that some will want to use this prodding as an opportunity to clarify their understandings, purposes, feelings, aspirations, attitudes, beliefs, and so on."[3]

This is not the place for questions to which you already have the answer, questions that ask "Why?" or "either-or" types. Raths provides a sample list categorized under the seven criteria of a value.[4] Here are a few selections for each heading:

Choosing freely: Where do you suppose you first got that idea? Are you the only one in your crowd who feels this way? What do your parents want you to be? Is there any rebellion in your choice?

Choosing from alternatives: How long did you look around before you decided? What choices did you reject before you settled on this one? What's really good about this choice that makes it stand out from the other possibilities?

Choosing thoughtfully and reflectively: What would be the consequences of each option? Are you implying that . . . [distort his statement to see if he is clear enough to correct the distortion]? If you do this, what will happen to . . . ? Is that consistent with what you said earlier? How would you rank these choices in the order of their importance?

Prizing and cherishing: Are you glad you feel that way? How do you feel about yourself when you do that? What good is it? Why is it important to you? In what way would life be different without it? Are you proud of the way you handled that situation?

Affirming: Would you tell the class the way you feel sometime? Are you saying that you believe . . . ? Do people know that you believe that way or that you do that thing? Are you willing to stand up and be counted for that?

Acting upon choices: What is your first step, second step, et cetera? Are you willing to put some of your money behind this idea? Have you done much reading on this topic? Where will this lead you? How far are you willing to go? How is this going to affect your life in the future?

Repeating: Have you felt this way for some time? Do you do this often? Will you get other people interested and involved? How long do you think you will continue? Will you do it again?

Caution! The authors of values clarification do not proceed from a religious framework and, indeed, have little to say about the *content* of values at all. If you have read the first section of this book, you will know that I consider both content and process to be vital in values formation. We will look at the criticisms of this approach in just a bit, but here I would like to point out that every one of the above questions can be applied easily to concerns involving religious principles and behavior. And questions with specific religious content can also be formulated. For example, If you knew Christ were coming tonight, what changes would you make in your life? How does watching TV affect your relationship with Christ? When they open the books in the great judgment day, what would you like your record to be most noted for? If you were arrested for being a Christian, upon what evidence could they convict you?

Some of the essential elements of a clarifying response are: (1) it avoids evaluating, (2) it puts the responsibility for thinking on the student, (3) it allows freedom not to respond, (4) it is not asked to obtain information but to stimulate clarification, (5) it is short and snappy, (6) it is directed primarily to an individual rather than a group, and (7) it has no "right" answer.[5]

Pros and Cons

The clarifying response and the other values clarification strategies that flow from it do not impose values, but they can be useful in stimulating young people to think about their positions on moral issues. This method assumes that young people often make important decisions without consciously considering how these decisions fit into their value system, and that, indeed, values of youth are likely to be rather hazy and not clearly integrated into a system at all.

Raths states: "You are not trying to change the ideas of students but to help them learn a process of thinking and valuing, so that they are less likely in the future to follow any persuasive leader blindly, to settle important ideas only on the basis of emotional preference, or to confuse thought with irrational approaches to vital issues."[6]

Some students of values education have criticized values clarification on a number of points, including (1) some of the seven processes seem unnecessary, (2) little help is provided when personal values conflict, and (3) it does not teach how to appraise your own and others' values critically.[7] More serious is the overemphasis on process to the neglect of content. The strategy seems to make all values equal and doesn't teach that some are better than others.

You may well ask, What if, after using values clarification methods, a child chooses an unacceptable value? Is it not possible that a youth might go through all seven of the criteria and come to value intolerance or thievery? Raths replies: "We respect his right to decide upon that value . . . but we must often deny him the right to carry the value to action. . . . It interferes too much with the freedom or rights of others." [8]

While this may be true as far as it goes, it does not go far enough. Simply to put youth through the process of value development without guidance as to the content of those values and then to restrain the carrying out of unacceptable values is not helping the child to lead a satisfying and productive life. Teaching and modeling those values that facilitate relationships with God and fellow humans is the wiser course—which is why chapter 6, "Choosing the Best Values," and chapter 13, "Learning Right From Wrong," were included earlier in this book. Fortunately, it is not an either-or proposition. Learning *how* to choose and learning *what* to choose can be effectively combined.

Raths lists a number of areas as rich in values clarification activities: money, friendship, love and sex, religion and morals, leisure, politics, work, family, maturity, and character traits. [9] Values in every one of these areas can and should be determined by religious considerations.

A Glimpse at Some Other Techniques

I have mentioned that the clarifying response leads into other values clarification exercises. One is the value sheet. The youth read or listen to a value-rich statement, write their personal reactions or answer questions based upon it, and finally discuss the piece. Since I consider this technique highly productive in stimulating value thinking, I would like to give several examples. They take up considerable space, so I'll save them for the next chapter.

Raths describes a number of additional techniques. [10]

We'll look at just a few, putting them in religious settings.

Role-playing or sociodrama. Students have a chance to put themselves in others' places and act out the values they believe those others have. Teachers may structure the situation: "You three fellows are going to try to get Jim here to join you in a 'pot party.' Jim, this is against your religious principles. Try, without condeming your friends, to explain why you can't participate."

The teacher can add new elements at any time. If Jim is having difficulty: "Sally, you're a friend of Jim's at church. He confides in you. Help him know how to answer the guys." It is probably better to call for volunteers for the parts, although to widen opportunity, the teacher may sometimes ask a student if he or she would be willing to assume a role.

Devil's advocate. Often young people have never considered objections to their values. Until they consider and answer these objections, their faith is not grounded very soundly. A teacher who takes the other side can banish apathy and make the students think. The teacher may set the stage: "I'm a Sundaykeeping preacher. I'm going to prove to you that the Ten Commandments were done away with at the cross. How will you answer my arguments?" After the students have become familiar with the technique, the teacher may launch into a devil's-advocate position without warning. This is sure to bring sloppy thinking up short.

The teacher may defend racially separated congregations, a ban on women's speaking publicly in religious services, having more than one wife, the use of alcoholic beverages, et cetera. Caution! Don't leave the students confused about where you stand. Don't be *too* persuasive at first, but tailor the strength of your objections to the growing ability of your students to combat them. Do insist that students find answers based on religious principles.

Reaction sheets. All through the day and week, young people find themselves in life situations that have value implications. One helpful strategy is to ask them to pick out a situation and react to it in writing as it concerns their values. The teacher may supply questions to guide the thinking (What, if anything, did you do this week of which you are proud?) or may leave the exercise open-ended. Students have reacted to the school picnic, a family discussion, a date, a worship service, and an assignment, among others.

One academy senior in my youth guidance class wrote about her feelings after attending the Saturday-night movie shown on campus: "When the hero punched the bad guy, I cheered along with all the other kids. But later I began to think. What is happening to me that I, a Christian, could be so glad to see another human getting hurt? Is this movie destroying my sensitivity to human worth?" She wrote a page along this line. It was one of the most effective value statements I have ever read, and it formed the basis for a thoughtful discussion with the class.

Open-ended questions. The teacher can write an open-ended question on the board and ask the students to write a response. This is a quickie that can be worked in between other things. Some examples: If I had only twenty-four hours to live . . . What I want most out of life is . . . When I think of the church, I . . . The quality I want most in a husband or wife is . . . People of other races . . . Jesus Christ is . . .

This method forces students to consider their values, and when the papers are collected, the teacher has the basis for a good discussion on morality.

Action projects. These consist of giving students opportunity to do something about an important issue. Some things that have been done: tutoring children in the ghetto, "adopting" a grandparent at a nursing home, holding a Bible Story Hour or Vacation Bible School for neighborhood children, collecting food and delivering it to hungry families, raising money to sponsor an overseas child in a Christian school. Acting on our values strengthens them.

These are only a few of the techniques that may be found in the Raths book and others. Most of the strategies will be usable for our purposes, but many of the specific questions, passages, and situations will not be adequate, because they are presented in a secular framework. However, it is fairly easy to fit religious material to the techniques, as I have tried to demonstrate in this chapter. Remember, it is not the method or even necessarily the content that distinguishes the Christian from the humanist. It is the perspective and the motivation.

In this chapter I have repeatedly used the term *teacher*. This is the way most of the exercises are written. But please understand that *teacher* may read *parent*, since the parent is the first and most influential of all teachers. Nearly all of these strategies can be adapted to home use. Now, on to Value Sheets!

Notes

[1] Raths et al., *Values and Teaching*, pp. 38, 39.

[2] Barbara Glaser and Howard Kirschenbaum, "Using Values Clarification in Counseling Settings," *The Personnel and Guidance Journal* 58 (May, 1980): 569-574.

[3] Raths et al., *op. cit.*, p. 80.

[4] *Ibid.*, pp. 63-65.

[5] *Ibid.*, pp. 53, 54.

[6] *Ibid.*, p. 190.

[7] Fraenkel, *How to Teach About Values*, pp. 42-47.

[8] Raths et al., *op. cit,.* p. 227.

[9] *Ibid.*, p. 260.

[10] *Ibid.*, pp. 112-162.

CHAPTER 18

The Value Sheet

After three dates and countless snatches of conversation between classes, Matt knew he was in love. Wandering downtown for three hours the week before Christmas, he searched for the perfect gift for Carrie.

He finally sauntered into a jewelry store and explained to the saleslady that he wanted a really nice present for his special girlfriend. She led him to a nearby display case and set a brown velvet box before him.

The moment he opened the box and saw that gold locket, Matt knew it was perfect. The gold glistened in the light—just like Carrie's eyes. It was expensive, but Matt had been saving a long time. He knew Carrie couldn't help loving it. So he paid for it, took it home, and very carefully wrapped it himself. That locket did make the perfect gift. Matt knew that as long as he lived he'd never forget the night he gave Carrie that gold locket.

Winter hadn't reached February before something happened to Matt's love. The warmth seemed to fade. Breaking up brought the greatest sense of sadness and loss Matt had ever known. But a few months later Matt met Rita, with dark flashing eyes and a fiery personality. Love struck again. Matt decided he wanted to show his love for Rita with a special gift.

He haunted the stores, trying to decide what to buy. But he always found himself back in the jewelry store, looking at the gold lockets. He wracked his brain for other ideas, but no other gift seemed as perfect. So he ended up giving Rita a locket. She thought it was beautiful.

Matt and Rita broke up a few months later. After Rita he dated Barb, and after Barb came Sandy and Arlene and then Nicole. He really cared about each one. Whenever a birthday or some other special occasion called for a special gift, he would return to the familiar jewelry store to buy another gold locket. A couple of times he felt a little guilty about not putting any more thought or effort into choosing a gift. But even when he tried, he couldn't think of a nicer present than that locket.

Finally Matt met Carol. Right away there was a different look about him when he was with her. He knew no one had ever understood or loved him the way Carol did. All his previous loves paled in the light of his love for her. No one was surprised when Matt asked Carol to marry him.

A few weeks before the big event Matt went to pick out a wedding gift. He wanted it to be special—symbolic of his love. He tried to think of something else, but he finally settled on that beautiful gold locket. Nothing else seemed quite as perfect as a means of expressing how he felt about Carol.

Their wedding was as exciting and beautiful as both of them had dreamed. And when the exhausting day of ceremony and festivity came to a close and the two of them were finally alone, Matt presented his gift to Carol.

She told him the locket was beautiful. She also said that he'd given her the happiest day and the most wonderful gift she'd ever had. But when Carol put on the locket, Matt couldn't help remembering all the other gold lockets he'd given. He wondered if Carol knew. He wished he could have given her something truly unique, for her alone.

Always before, that 24-karat gold locket had seemed such a perfect gift. But now, on the happiest day of his life, that locket didn't seem special or beautiful anymore. It didn't even look as gold as Matt remembered.

1. What does this story say to you personally?

2. As a Christian, what reasons do you have for wanting to give your wife or husband a unique gift?

3. What do you learn about the character of God?

4. What do you learn about the dignity and worth of people from this story?

5. What gift would you like to give on your wedding night?

The above material is an example of a value sheet. I condensed the story from *Campus Life*, April, 1978, pages 62-63, and supplied the questions. It could be printed out for the students, or it could be read orally with the questions written on the board. Obviously it is intended for the teenage level.

The value sheet consists of a provocative statement and a series of questions about it.[1] The purpose of the statement is to raise an issue that may have value implications (for us, it must have religious connections). The questions are first answered in writing and then used as a basis for large or small group discussion. Students need to grapple with the questions and do some independent thinking *before* getting involved in any discussion that might tempt them to avoid thinking for themselves and just to listen passively to others. Some characteristics of value sheets are:

1. The examples are controversial in some way.

2. The questions make large use of "you" and "your."

3. The questions allow for free discussion without "loading the dice."

4. The questions try to find out what young people really care about.

5. The questions strive to move youth to *do* something about their choices.

The parent or teacher should not moralize but allow the young people to discover and draw out the meanings. Questioning is more effective than lecturing. Of course, the adult may (and should) state his/her personal values, making it clear that the student should not accept them uncritically. It may be wise to withhold your personal values at the outset in order to give youth the chance to think for themselves without pressure.

The value sheet may make use of a variety of materials:

parables (such as "The Gold Locket"), an experience from a person's life, essays, opposing views on an issue (which statement most nearly represents your position?), passages from great literature, cartoons, poetry, music, articles in church papers, et cetera.

You can find the ingredients for value sheets everywhere. While articles from the religious press may be most obvious, an abundance of material from "secular" sources furnishes rich resources for religious applications. Let's try a few more.

ADVENTISTS AND DISARMAMENT
By Bert B. Beach

Dedicated Christians have been pacifists and crusaders, while on the other hand, fervent Marxists have been pacifists and militant revolutionaries. It is fully possible for devout Christians to perceive facts differently and reach diametrically opposed conclusions on sociopolitical questions such as those of war and peace. Church leaders lack access to all the information needed to make sound policy recommendations dealing with the issue. . . .

It appears self-evident that churches and their leaders do not have the expertise to measure national security. They have no access to classified information and intelligence reports. They have no expert knowledge regarding armaments and military capacity. They know next to nothing about the dense-packing of MX missiles, and not much more about the balance of power. This being the case, it is hardly appropriate for church officials to act as experts and speak out regarding government defense and security policy. What churchmen can and must do—however, with great care and circumspection—is deal with moral principles and implications from a biblical perspective.[2]

1. What is your position on nuclear weapons?

2. What are the biblical and moral reasons for your position?

3. Do you think that any circumstances could justify a nation engaging in nuclear warfare? If so, when?

4. Do you see disarmament as primarily a sociopolitical question, or is it a matter of religious principle?

5. In your opinion, should the church as an official body speak out on this issue? Why?

6. What are you willing to do to support your convictions on war and peace?

INVINCIBLE TOWN
By Arnold Kurtz

Years ago I served as a colonel in the Austrian Army. I was commanded to march against a little town in the Tyrol and lay siege to it. My confidence in the success of the venture was dampened by a remark from a prisoner we had taken. "You will never take that town, for they have an invincible leader." . . . I doubled my preparations in case there should be some truth in the report.

As we descended through the pass in the Alps, I saw with surprise that the cattle were still grazing in the valley and that women and children and even the men were working in the fields. Either they are not expecting us or this is a trap, I thought to myself. As we drew nearer the town, we passed people on the road. They smiled and greeted us with a friendly word, and then went on their way.

Finally we reached the town and clattered up the cobble-paved streets—colors flying, trumpets sounding a challenge, arms in readiness. It was impossible to keep strict discipline. . . . My soldiers answered the questions of the children, and I saw one old warrior throw a kiss to a little golden-haired tot on a doorstep. . . . Still no sign of ambush. We rode straight to the open square that faced the town hall. Here, if anywhere, resistance surely was to be expected.

As I reached the hall . . . an old white-haired man, who by his insignia I surmised to be the mayor, stepped forward. He walked down the steps straight to my horse's side, and with hand extended cried, "Welcome, brother!"

"Where are your soldiers?" I demanded.

"Soldiers? Why, don't you know we have none?" he replied in wonderment.

"But we have come to take this town."

"Well, no one will stop you."

"Are there none here to fight?"

At this question, the old man's face lighted up with a rare smile that I will always remember. His words were simple: "No, there is no one here to fight. We have chosen Christ for our leader, and He teaches another way."

There seemed nothing left for us to do but to ride away, leaving the town unmolested. . . . I reported to headquarters that it had offered unassailable resistance, although this admission injured my military reputation. But I was right. We had literally been conquered by these simple folk who followed implicitly the teachings of Christ.[3]

1. In a world stockpiled with military armaments, do you find this story too simplistic? Could this method work in the last quarter of the twentieth century?

2. How would you compare and contrast this article with the previous one by Bert Beach? What ideas are similar? What ideas are different?

3. As a Christian, how do you feel about the people who live in "enemy" countries?

4. Do you think a Christian is justified in defending his country? His family? His rights? What scriptural principles apply?

5. What can you do to bring peace into the conflicts you meet in your environment?

TO SPEAK OR NOT TO SPEAK
Pastor Martin Niemöller

In Germany they came first for the Communists, and I didn't speak up because I wasn't a Communist. Then they came for the Jews, and I didn't speak up because I wasn't a Jew. Then they came for the trade unionists, and I didn't speak up because I wasn't a trade unionist. Then they came for the Catholics, and I didn't speak up because I was a

Protestant. Then they came for me, and by that time no one was left to speak up.[4]

1. To you, what is the central meaning of this statement?

2. What is the pastor *for* and what is he *against?*

3. When would they have come for you?

4. Are some things going on in our world right now about which, as a Christian, you might need to speak up? List them.

5. Should a Christian be concerned about what happens to Communists, Jews, Moslems, Buddhists, et cetera? Why?

6. How does a Christian go about speaking up? What ways are appropriate?

7. Should a Christian have a concern for social justice or merely for individual conversions? How does your understanding of God affect your answer?

LAMBS TO THE SLAUGHTER
By Dennis Crews

In 1976 a women's rally in Rome made the declaration "The body is not to be managed by the doctor, and even less by God. The womb is mine, and I manage it myself." Such a blatant statement of independence from the Creator is startling at first reading, but it expresses perfectly the essence of a decision for abortion. One of the favorite slogans bandied about by pro-abortionists is "Every woman has the right to control her own body."

This slogan is pathetically inappropriate when dealing with a pregnant body. Neither science nor medicine will permit the folly of ignoring the fact that in pregnancy there are two bodies. Regardless of the lack of value one may accord the smaller body, it exists as a wholly separate and unique biological entity, even though surrounded and transported by the larger one. Is there a moral distinction between smashing the head of a baby a half hour old and using a saline injection to kill the same baby a half hour before birth?

Christians ought to be the most vocal defenders of those little people who are eliminated simply for being inconvenient. Just being alive and in Christ places this responsibility upon us.[5]

1. How does your understanding of God's character influence your position on abortion?

2. Do you find any guidance in Scripture as to when human life begins?

3. Does Dennis Crews overstate the prolife case for dramatic effect? In what ways?

4. As a Christian, could you have an abortion or counsel someone else to have one under certain circumstances? What circumstances?

5. Should the church take an official position on abortion, or should it be left a personal matter between the Christian and God?

Space forces me to stop, but these examples show how readily you can stimulate moral reasoning with value sheets. I have found this tool to be one of the most effective in values education.

Notes

[1] Raths et al., *Values and Teaching*, pp. 83-86.

[2] Excerpted from *Adventist Review*, April 21, 1983, pp. 4, 5.

[3] Condensed from *Adventist Review*, May 24, 1979, p. 10.

[4] In Raths et al., *op. cit.*, p. 105.

[5] Excerpted from *The Inside Report From Amazing Facts*, February, 1984, pp. 1, 2, 7.

CHAPTER 19

Value Reasoning

All men are human beings. Debbie Martin is a human being. Therefore, Debbie Martin is a man.

Did my loose logic cause you to do a double-take? That was just to get your attention, but in fact, many people do not know how to move from accepted premise to sound conclusion in a logical manner. This can be a particularly serious problem when it concerns moral reasoning.

We have already noted that a serious criticism of values clarification is that it concentrates on the process of developing values without attempting to influence *what* values will be developed. While we have seen that young people must choose their values for themselves and we cannot impose our values on our children, yet we want them to choose the best values.

The Association for Values Education and Research (AVER) has developed an approach that attempts to combine moral reasoning with the content of abstract universal values. This method is called *value reasoning*.[1]

Learning Skills

AVER has identified a number of learning skills/activities that appear to be important in learning how to reason about values. I'll scan them and set them in a religious framework.

Factual claims/value judgments. Factual claims are statements that are true or false by definition (religion is the explanation of life in terms of ultimate meanings) or on the basis of evidence (the majority of Adventists in North

America are females). Factual refers to the kind of statement that can be clarified by definition or empirically tested, rather than to its truth or falsity. Incorrect statements may be factual claims.

Value judgments are statements that rate things with respect to their worth. The ratings may be positive, negative, or neutral. They imply a value principle behind the judgment. A judgment might be "People of all races should worship and fellowship together." The implied principle is the equal dignity and worth of all humans before God. A *definitional* value judgment is a generalized assertion about the quality or worth of something (the Adventist teaching on death is a very comforting one). A *propositional* judgment indicates that someone should do something (the church should change its stance on the ordination of women). It is important to be able to distinguish between a factual claim and a value judgment.

Value sentences. Value judgments or value sentences contain both *value objects* and *value terms.* Value objects are what is being evaluated. In the judgment "Drugs are dangerous," the object is drugs. But we need to define both objects and terms. What is included in the object "drugs"? Does it include all drugs, or only illegal, "street" drugs? And what qualifies as a drug?

Likewise with the term that evaluates the worth of the object. Dangerous in what way? What do we mean by good or bad, right or wrong, beautiful or ugly, should or should not? This skill calls for us to be precise in formulating our value sentences.

Points of view. Value judgments may be made from a number of different points of view: moral, aesthetic, health and safety, economic, prudential, environmental, and religious. These refer to the kind of reasons needed to justify the judgment. A judgment and the reasons supporting it should be made from the same point of view. In the statement "We should not steal someone else's things because we may be sent to jail," a moral judgment is being supported by a prudential reason. The teacher can help the youth search for moral and religious reasons.

Role taking. Role-taking activities in value reasoning are organized so that the participant gains information about the experience, the feelings, the ideas, et cetera, of other persons involved in the situation under consideration. We discussed this method briefly in chapter 17. Fraenkel suggests the following guidelines: (1) warm up by presenting the dilemma to the point where the decision is to be made; (2) select the role players; (3) prepare the rest of the class as observers, assigning observer tasks; (4) set the stage, give players time to plan and to assemble props; (5) enact the situation; (6) discuss, evaluate, and debrief; (7) replay the scene differently or with different players; (8) have further discussion; and (9) draw conclusions, but do not dictate how youth should feel.² By putting himself imaginatively into the role of another, a youth may come to appreciate the consequences of an action or an attitude for that person.

Reasons assembly chart. This is simply a device to gather as many relevant facts as possible from which to make a particular value judgment. A column for positive facts and a column for negative facts is provided on the chart. Sources for facts include Scripture, personal belief, authoritative opinion (one must evaluate how competent the "experts" are), observation, documentation, and experimentation. The facts supporting each side of the issue are then ranked in terms of their importance to the adolescent involved, and a judgment is made. A Christian teenager might use this method to decide on choosing a certain vocation or whether to date a particular member of the opposite sex.

Practical syllogism. This structure from formal logic consists of three elements. An example: "All human beings deserve to be treated with respect. Juvenile delinquents are human beings. Therefore, juvenile delinquents deserve to be treated with respect." The first element, called the major premise, is always a value principle. (All human beings deserve to be treated with respect.) The second element, or minor premise, is a factual claim (Juvenile delinquents are human beings). The third element, or conclusion, is the value judgment (Therefore, juvenile delinquents deserve to be treated with respect).

Logical reasoning here demands that three questions be satisfactorily answered: 1. Is the value principle acceptable? This is determined by the skill of principle testing, to be described next. 2. Is the factual claim true? 3. Does the conclusion follow logically from the major and the minor premise? A Yes answer to the third question makes a valid argument, but the conclusion may still not be true unless the first two questions also evoke Yes answers.

Principle testing. While a factual claim may be found to be true or false on the basis of evidence or of meaning, value judgments are judged to be acceptable or unacceptable on the validity of the value principle implied by the judgment. Determining the acceptability of a value judgment requires the testing of the value principle through a series of principle tests.

"In the role exchange test, participants are asked to identify the persons significantly affected by the judgment, especially those who are most adversely affected; to imagine the consequences of the judgment for those most adversely affected; and to determine if they would accept the consequences of that judgment if they themselves were the most adversely affected." [3]

This sounds very much like the golden rule. In testing the principle "All human beings deserve to be treated with respect," the youth may be asked to confront the question If I were a prisoner, on welfare, or a member of a minority ethnic group, how would I wish to be treated?

The universal consequences test asks the question But what if everyone did that? What would the consequences be if everyone engaged in a certain action, such as throwing cans and garbage out of the car window? Would the consequences be acceptable? Suppose everyone supported foreign missions to the extent that I do? "This test is based on the principle of respect for persons, which requires that all persons be treated the same unless there are good reasons for treating them differently." [4] Consequences may be established by noting historical parallels, if available, or by trying to predict on the basis of other knowns. The teacher is a resource person who introduces overlooked consequences.

The new cases test applies the principle used in a value judgment to similar relevant cases. If the principle proposed is People should never steal, then this principle would be fitted to a number of situations to determine if one is willing to apply the principle consistently. We might ask if a starving family would be justified in stealing food in order to survive, or if one should steal a weapon from a violent person who was planning to use it to harm others. If a value principle will not apply to all new cases, it is rejected or modified somewhat.

The subsumption test is based on the idea that a value principle is acceptable if it follows logically from another value principle of a higher order. Thus the value principle that men and women are equal rather than one being subservient to the other may follow from the principle that God created both male and female in His own image.

Thus value reasoning as a technique does not impose value judgments on students but provides them a way of examining value systems objectively. At the same time it focuses on those broad, abstract value principles that are important to family life educators—justice, equality, social responsibility.

Related Exercises

Fraenkel suggests a slightly different approach to a values reasoning process. He believes that students should be given opportunities to:

1. Suggest various ways they would react in situations involving another person.

2. Work out possible consequences of an action on both themselves and others.

3. Identify how they and others would feel in various

types of situations.

4. Take on the role of another person.

5. Identify alternative courses of action that might be pursued in various situations.

6. Evaluate various alternatives from several points of view (legal, economic, aesthetic, prudential, moral, health, et cetera).

7. Assess predicted consequences of proposed alternative policies or actions in terms of both the likelihood and the desirability of their occurrence.[5]

One way to do this would be to analyze a value conflict.[6] The teacher presents a value dilemma—a situation in which conflict is present—and follows with a series of probing questions: What are the facts of the dilemma? Is the conflict over ends or means? What alternatives are open? Can you predict the consequences of the various alternatives? What might happen to those not immediately involved (both long- and short-range consequences should be considered)? What evidence is there that the predicted consequences would occur (search for data)? Would each consequence be good or bad? Why (set up criteria)? What is the best decision? How would you rank choices from the most desirable to the least desirable?

Fraenkel suggests that questions focusing on values may be of three types:

1. *Factual type:* Asks for names, dates, places, events, and descriptions. Answers can be verified by observation.

2. *Definitional type:* Asks for characteristics, examples, and meanings. No "correct" answers, but more or less "agreed-on" answers.

3. *Inferential type:* Asks for conclusions, alternatives, generalizations, values, feelings, and hypotheses. Many possible answers.[7]

Since a young person must have a foundation of factual data before he or she can make responsible inferences about values or discuss moral dilemmas, it is important to seek answers for all three types of questions. Learning to reason morally is every bit as challenging a task as learning to reason mathematically or scientifically.

Notes

[1] Margaret Edwards Arcus, "Values Reasoning: An Approach to Value Education," *Family Relations* 29 (April, 1980): 163-171.

[2] Fraenkel, *How to Teach About Values*, pp. 109-112.

[3] Arcus, *op. cit.*, p. 170.

[4] *Ibid.*

[5] Fraenkel, *op. cit.*, p. 106.

[6] *Ibid.*, pp. 126-134.

[7] *Ibid.*, pp. 86-89.

CHAPTER 20

Potpourri

A nuclear attack has just occurred! Thousands in your city are dead or dying. But a radiation-proof shelter has space and supplies for seven people to find safety until the danger from fallout is past. The problem is that ten candidates show up and request admittance. It is your responsibility to decide which seven can come in and thus survive and which three must stay out and perish. What are your choices? On what basis do you make them? The candidates:

1. A bookkeeper, 31 years old
2. His wife, six months pregnant
3. A black militant, second-year medical student
4. A famous historian-author, 42 years old
5. A Hollywood starlet (singer and dancer), 25 years old
6. A homosexual biochemist, 37 years old
7. A minister, 59 years old
8. A college coed, 19 years old (has never had a date)
9. An Olympic track star, 22 years old
10. A policeman with his gun, 48 years old

   This exercise has a number of variations (such as who gets on a life raft when the ship is sinking), and the cast of characters can be changed to reflect any combination of virtues and vices. It is best used as a group technique with the group being forced to come to a consensus within a limited amount of time. Each young person argues for his/her candidates and is exposed to the reasoning of those who support different choices. Selections imply values, of course, and the participants are required to confront those human values that may have been only vague in their thinking prior to the exercise. Afterward the youth may be questioned as to what religious principles guided them in their selections.

In previous chapters in this section we have looked at major approaches to transmitting values, such as using moral dilemmas, values clarification, the value sheet, and value reasoning. In this chapter we shall consider a potpourri of techniques that are related to, but somewhat different from, the major methods.

Exploring Feelings

Values have a strong emotional component. Teachers should encourage and help students participate in experiences that allow them to feel many different kinds of emotions, to contact many different kinds of people, to do different things, and then to share their perceptions of and feelings about these experiences. Fraenkel lists twenty-three typical experiences. Several with possible religious overtones are:

1. Visit a home for the aged.
2. Give someone a flower every day for a week.
3. Listen to a tape recording of Martin Luther King's "I Have a Dream" speech.
4. Try to go without food for a whole day.
5. Talk to a blind person about what it's like to be blind.
6. Volunteer some time to help patients in a hospital.
7. Take your mom (or dad) for a walk.
8. Interview someone at the animal shelter as to how many unwanted animals the shelter must dispose of in a year and how the disposal is done.
9. Write a poem about love.[1]

After the youth have participated in the experience, they should be encouraged to talk about how they felt and why. Other questions are How did others feel? What conclusions can you draw about how people feel in situations like this? How is this activity an outworking of your religious faith? This exercise increases awareness of how people who may seem different outwardly are really like us in their basic makeup. Thus it elevates our view of the dignity and worth of humanity.

Growing With Television

Television is undoubtedly one of the greatest purveyors of values in contemporary society. Much of it is negative from a Christian point of view. Some parents react by banning it from their homes. But it is not realistic to think that one can isolate his children from so ubiquitous an influence. Another approach is for parents and children together to examine and discuss the values being telecast into their living rooms.

Parents may find a helpful tool for this task in *Growing With Television: A Study of Biblical Values and the Television Experience,* published in 1980 by the Media Action Research Center, Room 1370, 475 Riverside Drive, New York 10115. This resource provides a twelve-session workshop on the values of television from a biblical perspective. It was funded by a grant from the Episcopal Church.

Leaders' guides and student leaflets are provided for five different age levels (younger elementary, older elementary, junior high, senior high, and adult). A few of the twelve sessions are "Simplistic Problems and Solutions," "Real/Not Real," "Images of Others," and "Sex and Sexuality."

Positive Description

For a class, this is a good exercise in affirmation. Each member is asked to write a description of the good qualities of some other person in the room. Emphasize spiritual characteristics, caring for others, and unique personality traits. Then each student is given opportunity to read his/her description aloud, and the rest of the group try to guess who is being described. This technique helps create a sense of community in the group, reinforces other-centered qualities, and leads to an appreciation of the unique worth of other human beings.

Lifeline Poster

Each member of the class creates a lifeline poster, which is a large sheet of poster board that includes a chronology of the significant people, places, and events in one's life from birth to the present time. Youth can especially portray the mileposts on their spiritual pilgrimage, such as conversion, baptism, camp meetings, encounters with God, witnessing adventures, church responsibilities, et cetera. Members explain their lifelines to each other and are encouraged to ask questions and make comments.

Value Ranking

The adolescent is given a list of values and asked to rank them in the order of their priority to the ranker.[2] Then the youth is provided with previously obtained information designed to increase self-awareness about possibly chronic contradictions existing within himself/herself (1) between two or more personal values, (2) between values and attitudes, or (3) between values and behaviors. The confrontation is by the Socratic method, with the young people allowed to discover the contradictions for themselves. This process leads to a state of self-dissatisfaction that is assumed to initiate desire for change. Studies have shown changes both in attitudes and behaviors as a result of this method, which persisted when measured as long as twenty-one months later.

While adolescents may be presented with simply a list of value words (wisdom, happiness, freedom, salvation, et cetera), an interesting variation makes use of fanciful descriptions. For example, "The Specialists" describes thirteen suppliers of services that one might wish to patronize:

1. Dr. Happy Face: A noted plastic surgeon. He can make you look exactly as you want to look by means of a new painless technique (he also uses hormones to alter body structures and size). Your ideal physical appearance can be a reality.

2. Prince Jobber: A college placement and job placement expert. The college or job of your choice, in the location of your choice, will be yours (he also provides immunity from the draft, if you wish).

3. Further Time: Guarantees you long life (to the age of 200), with your aging processes slowed down proportionately. For example, at the age of 60 you will look and feel like 20.

4. Drs. Misters and Jackson: Experts in the area of sexual relations, they guarantee that you will be the perfect male or female, will enjoy sex, and will always bring pleasure to your mate.

5. Dr. Exo Cize: He will provide you with perfect health and with protection from physical injury as long as you live.

6. Goody Friend: He guarantees that you will have the friends you want now and in the future. You will find it easy to approach those you like, and they will find you easily approachable.

7. Al Brain: He will develop your common sense and your intelligence to an IQ level in excess of 150. It will remain at that level throughout your entire lifetime.

8. Lotta Money: Wealth will be yours, with guaranteed schemes for earning millions within weeks.

9. I. M. Right: This world-famous leadership expert will train you quickly. You will be listened to, looked up to, and respected by those around you.

10. Dr. I. Will Care: You will be well liked by all and will never be lonely. A life filled with love will be yours.

11. Dr. Seesall: All of your questions about the future will be answered continually through the training of this soothsayer.

12. I. M. Perfect: Guarantees that you will have self-knowledge, self-liking, self-respect, and self-confidence. True self-assurance will be yours.

13. Will B. Clear: With his help you will always know what you want, and you will be completely clear on all the muddy issues of these confused days.

If you were allowed to choose any two of these, which two would it be? What are the reasons for your choices? What Christian principles guided you in making your choices? Does Scripture provide any guidelines for weighing these values? How do each of these suppliers enhance your relationships with God and with other humans?

Of course, no magic supplier exists who can hand out these values instantly. And yet, people do devote their lives to seeking the values that they represent. This exercise forces young people to look at what is most important to them. The follow-up questions challenge them to ask themselves if those values are what they really want to be most important.

Value Auction

For this class activity the students are supplied with a value auction sheet and "$5,000" each. Some of the values may be a satisfying and fulfilling marriage, freedom to do what I want, a long life free of illness, success in my chosen vocation, a satisfying religious faith, and a chance to eliminate sickness and poverty (Smith lists twenty-two values). [3]

A column marked "highest amount I bid" helps participants recall their interest in various items. When an item is sold, the highest bid is recorded by everyone, along with the initials of the person who bought it. Each participant can bid on and buy as many items as his/her bank balance will allow. A variation is to give each participant a number of tokens that can be used to purchase values until the tokens run out. Each value can end up with only one person.

The valuable part of this exercise is the discussion following the auction. Are you happy with what you got? Why did you spend your money the way you did? If you were to do it over again, what would you do differently? Young people are brought to realize that one can't have everything in life. Whatever we choose cuts out something else. Therefore, it is important to set priorities. Religious values should guide this priority setting.

This chapter has merely sampled the possible techniques to aid in stimulating the development of a value system. Many books give detailed descriptions of dozens of them. Smith covers twenty-nine strategies, including several I have discussed.[4] It is difficult to credit sources in this field because the same or similar approaches appear in many different works, and it is not at all certain who originated a particular idea.

However, most strategies will not be set in a Christian, or even a religious, framework. They have been prepared for the public schools and take a secular approach to moral education. I have tried to demonstrate that it is relatively easy to use the method but put the problem in terms of a religious issue and focus the follow-up questions on religious values.

Notes

[1] Fraenkel, *How to Teach About Values,* pp. 107-109.

[2] Milton Rokeach and John F. Regan, ''The Role of Values in the Counseling Situation,'' *The Personnel and Guidance Journal* 58 (May, 1980): 580.

[3] Maury Smith, *A Practical Guide to Value Clarification* (LaJolla, Calif.: University Associates, 1977), pp. 25-29.

[4] *Ibid.,* pp. 19-161.

CHAPTER 21

Show Me the Way

We stood in line in the gathering twilight, waiting for the doors to open for the evening program. At the front of the line was a chattering group of students who attended the academy where I was teaching. Then stood several of the faculty members with their respective spouses.

Just ahead of me a teacher shivered in the chilly evening air. He reached out and playfully pulled his wife close to him. "I'm glad I've got someone here to keep me warm," he announced to those of us in the immediate vicinity. I chuckled at the happy smile on his face and the exaggerated snuggle.

In front of him, however, a female staff member turned around and took in the situation. She did not chuckle. "How are you going to explain this to the students?" she questioned.

"No problem," replied the snuggler. "I've got a marriage license."

The lady paused a moment. She apparently didn't want to be disagreeable, but she had some convictions. "I just can't agree with that reasoning," she said. "We shouldn't do openly what we won't allow the students to do."

Fortunately, the doors opened just then. Attention was diverted to moving on inside. A possible crisis was averted. And I was left with some deep thoughts.

To what degree, if any, should married people display signs of affection in the presence of others? Will these endearments prove to be a sight too stimulating for unmarried young people such as students or their own children? Will they put ideas into the students' heads and call forth emotions that they are not yet mature enough to handle? Or does such tenderness provide a model from which youth can formulate their standards of what it means to be a loving spouse and thus prepare them to function as partners in happy marriages?

Importance of Modeling

Throughout this book I have repeatedly stressed the importance of modeling in moral development. Special focus was provided in the chapters on social learning theory and on the report of research on values transmission. Though I have described and recommended a number of techniques, no technique is as important as modeling. Modeling is not a strategy to be applied in a given situation like the other approaches. It is a way of living. As a matter of fact, none of the techniques in this book are particularly helpful without appropriate models. They stimulate youth to think through and choose values, but the young people must see what Christian values look like before they can choose them.

The term *modeling* is often used to indicate that the adult should set a good example in specific behaviors, such as attending church, abstaining from alcohol and tobacco, being faithful to his/her spouse, paying an honest income tax, et cetera. Of course, this is true. But beyond these specifics, how does an adult model the universal, abstract, cosmic values? How can you and I, by the lives we live, make it more likely that the young people within our sphere of influence will choose those values that facilitate relationships between themselves and God and between themselves and other humans?

In view of the perspective from which I have written, it seems fitting that this final chapter should attempt some principles of modeling for relational values. I will choose three as representative—love for family, the dignity and worth of people, and relationship with God.

Love for Family

"God is love" (1 John 4:8), and "love is the fulfillment of the law" (Rom. 13:10). Therefore, no religious value can exceed love in importance. While love is broad enough to encompass the world, it finds special definition in the marriage relationship (Eph. 5:22-33) and, by extension, to the family.

Love is not merely a warm feeling, though the behaviors of love do tend to generate positive emotions. Love is a decision to seek the good of the loved one. Rollo May defines love as "a delight in the presence of the other person and an affirming of his value and development as much as one's own." [1] Love, then, is always active. It reveals itself in behaviors designed to express the worth of the loved one and to meet his/her physical, psychological, social, and emotional needs.

"We receive love," writes May, "not in proportion to our demands or sacrifices or needs, but roughly in proportion to our own capacity to love. . . . To love means, essentially, to give." [2] God personifies love because He personifies giving (John 3:16).

Christian love is unconditional. It does not base its favors on the merits of the loved one, but continues to love in spite of unworthiness in the other. This is the way God loves us (Rom. 5:6-8). And it is the way God wants us to love Him. May quotes Spinoza thus: "Whoso loveth God truly must not expect to be loved by Him in return." [3] Not that God does not love us, but the philosopher has captured the deep principle that love given in hopes of a return is not love at all.

This is also the way we are to love people. The command of Jesus to love "without expecting to get anything back" (Luke 6:32-35) has special significance in the family. Our Christian values will cause us to demonstrate loving, caring behavior toward our spouses and our children even when they are not lovable and do not do the things we would like them to do. Such a modeling of unselfish concern for others will have a powerful effect on the youth. They will compare Christian love with the brand that the world has to offer (exploitation) and may well decide that the parental value is too precious to discard.

Now how does this apply to the questions raised by our opening illustration? The Christian marriage contains much affection. It is filled with both verbal endearments and nonverbal communications of caring. Ellen White counsels that "a home where love dwells and where it finds expression in looks, in words, in acts, is a place where angels delight to dwell." [4] But love must be demonstrated to survive. "The plant of love must be carefully nourished, else it will die." [5] "There is need of expressing love and tenderness in a chaste, pure, dignified way." [6]

But how do children learn that this is what they should do when they reach adulthood and set up their own homes? By what they have seen in the family. Children learn the roles of husband and wife from what they have observed in their own parents. Thus in God's wise plan a young person who grows up in a warm, loving home is continually learning the role that he or she will someday enact.

Children early get the message that their parents adore each other. Their ears are filled with the words of appreciation, sweet pet names, and the soft tones that parents exchange. They notice the smile on Dad's face and the sparkle in Mom's eyes as they gaze at each other. Youthful minds register the thoughtful little acts that one parent does for another. Children are impressed by the patience and kindness with which Mom and Dad address each other in stressful situations. They often see their parents holding hands or with arms entwined.

And what about outside the home? Many adolescents have not grown up in the presence of a loving marriage. For them the modeling of a teacher or pastor and spouse may be the second chance to learn about building a happy Christian home. Of course the couple will use discretion. The more intimate displays of affection will be reserved for privacy. But the little, meaningful signs can be there, and they can be seen with profit by young onlookers.

Physical demonstrations of affection are also needed by children. Much research has shown the need of human beings for touching. When parents frequently hug and cuddle their children, they not only help them to develop a healthy emotional life, but they also model what being a loving parent is like. A friend of mine in overseas mission service wrote me some reflections on his childhood that I would like to share:

"On my mother's part, even the goodbye and hello kiss was the exception when we were children. I can still remember going to youth camp for the first time at age 14. I remember going to the front door upon returning home and ringing the bell so as to get a special welcome. Mother had been running the carpet sweeper and stopped to answer the door. When she saw me through the screen door, she said, 'Well, when did you get back? Why are you standing out there? Why don't you come in, silly?' As she returned to her sweeping I'm sure she must have said, 'Welcome home,' but having been away from home for the first time, I really was starving for a big hug and kiss from my mother, who in a thousand other ways proved that she loved me but simply did not know how to demonstrate any of that love through body contact.

"When she was 83 and I felt that I should make the ten-thousand-mile trip home to care for some of her needs, the same little drama was reenacted. The welcome was as if I had just returned from work, having left earlier that same day. As I finally grabbed her frail body and hugged and kissed it, I could sense a certain embarrassment that she did not know how to handle. Let's teach our children that there is a vital type of demonstration that brings health and is necessary for the survival of home and family."

This man was fortunate to find a "second chance" in good models among friends and an affectionate wife. But obviously the pain of his loss still persists after all these years. Loving parents will produce loving children and, someday, loving adults.

The Dignity and Worth of People

The Christian who believes in the fatherhood of God must also accept the brotherhood of mankind. Since all humans were created in the image of God, all have intrinsic value. One of the highest values that we wish our children to possess is respect for the dignity and worth of people. The second great commandment is to "love your neighbor as yourself" (Matt. 22:39).

The transmission of this value is very much related to good adult modeling. While we may—and should—teach this truth, demonstrating it in daily living is what is needed most. We affirm the importance of this principle when we treat our children with respect. The wise parent will not yell at children, insult them, slap them, imply that they are stupid, or put them down in any other way. While parents will need to apply correction and discipline from time to time, these should always be administered in a manner that preserves the self-worth of the young person.

Parents also model respect by taking their children seriously, listening to them, and soliciting their ideas on family concerns. People tend to treat others the way their parents treated them during their childhood. If their parents regarded them in a way that signified they were important, worthwhile beings, they will usually assimilate those principles and behave in a like manner toward others.

The same is true in the classroom. A mother told me about an experience her daughter had with a certain teacher. One day during class the instructor called on her for a bit of information. The girl was usually a good student, but this time, under the pressure of other tasks, she had not studied her lesson and did not know the answer. She was quite flustered. At the end of the period the teacher asked to see her for a minute. She thought he was going to reprimand her. Instead, he apologized and said he had not meant to embarrass her before the class. She came home praising this teacher and with a new sense of how a life can be influenced by a simple act of respect and caring.

We affirm the dignity and worth of people by our humor. Adults who wish to transmit this value will not tell jokes that denigrate Blacks, Polish, Italians, Jews, or other ethnic groups. Neither will they find them funny when others tell them. They will not accept stereotypes such as "Blacks are irresponsible," "Latins are lazy," "Germans are ruthless," or "women are illogical," but will insist that each individual be evaluated on his/her unique merits. They will not use or encourage so-called funny statements about the inadequacies of the opposite sex—especially those that cast the sacred institution of marriage in anything other than the highest light. They will never employ humor at the expense of their spouses and have no truck for mother-in-law jokes.

They view persons of the opposite sex not as objects to use for their pleasure but as human beings with feelings, mind, and character. They do not "use" people, but rather serve them. They see in every man a brother and in every woman a sister. They follow Christ, who "bowed with tenderest regard to every member of the family of God" [7] and who "in every human being, however fallen, . . . beheld a son of God." [8]

We also affirm the dignity and worth of people by our tolerance of differences. Adults who wish to transmit this value will not rant and rave against other denominations or religious groups. While they are not apologetic for their own beliefs, they freely allow that others have just as much right to teach and practice theirs. They acknowledge the fact that just because some disagree with them does not make these others inferior or bad. They know that sincere people may be mistaken and that even insincere people are still important to God.

This tolerance extends beyond religion. They respect people who differ with them on politics or economics or church policies. They do not look down on those who have less education or fewer possessions than they do, or who hold a less prestigious job. They see beyond the outward husk to the kernel of intrinsic worth placed within by creation and potential redemption. When parents and teachers live this kind of a lifestyle, youth have an excellent probability of developing the value of the worth and dignity of people.

Sometimes it may be necessary to take a forceful stand for a value, as Jesus did when He drove the money changers from the Temple. When I joined the faculty of a certain academy, I discovered that one of my duties was to lead the senior class on a weekend spiritual retreat at a beautiful lakeside setting. In addition to the meetings a number of recreational activities were planned. As the many preparations went forward, I heard a rumor that one of the "fun" things was for some of the bigger boys to throw other students into the lake after Sabbath. I assembled the seniors a few days before departure and said something like this:

"We want this experience to be both fun and a high point in our relationship with the Lord. We've provided for many recreational activities. But as Christians, we never want to have fun at someone else's expense. Now I have no objection if, at the right time, those who wish to, assemble and throw each other into the lake. I will even put on my swimsuit and let you throw me in. But I insist that no one be forced to participate against his or her will. I feel so strongly about this that I will immediately send anyone who violates my request back to the school."

The students were surprised at this stand because I had usually been quite democratic. A few grumbled. "Oh, come on. We were just going to have a little fun. We wouldn't hurt anybody."

"The cold water and wet clothes might make someone sick. Someone could get injured in the struggle. Or some might be terrified of water. But that's not the major point," I continued. "Each person is entitled to respect. When we physically force someone to do what he doesn't wish to do, we take away his control over his own body. We violate his person. That's not funny. It's a serious statement of his worth. Our purpose as Christians is to affirm personal dignity, not to violate it."

"Then let those who don't wish to be thrown in stay away from the lakeside," suggested one boy.

"No," I replied. "They have just as much right there as anyone else. They can sit on the dock or ride in the boats. In a Christian community none should have to hide to protect himself. We will all protect them because we value them."

Afterward, several students who hesitated to speak up in the group came to me privately and thanked me for my stand. The weekend proved to be a memorable one in the school calendar both spiritually and in terms of Christian fellowship. I regard the experience as among my most effective teaching.

Relationship with God

Admittedly it is more difficult to model relationship with God than to model the other values because of the private nature of this vertical fellowship. Nevertheless, let us attempt a brief description.

These adults live a life of basic trust. They "know that in all things God works for the good of those who love him" (Rom. 8:28). Therefore, they are not anxious about where the money will come from to pay the bills or about their health or their jobs or their future. Not that they let things slide. They are responsible and conscientious. But having done their best, they are willing to leave the results with God. They have their share of life's problems, but they do not complain. Rather, they are often found expressing gratitude for God's gracious gifts.

Models of this type make it clear that they are not earning their own salvation. They do not portray the Christian life as a series of duties that must be accomplished by stern perseverance. Neither do they picture it as a list of prohibitions that must be shunned by sheer willpower. They do not go about moaning as to their inability to measure up. While they confess that they are sinners, they are not paralyzed with guilt, for they have committed their salvation to Jesus Christ. They believe that He has forgiven their sins and that they are clothed with the robe of His righteousness. They daily invite the Holy Spirit to control their lives, and they believe that God is working out His character in them.

Their Christian walk, then, is not in long-faced solemnity but in joy. They freely choose the life of faith; they prize and cherish it; they live it out. They are happy to share their experience with others, and they do so, not like a high-pressure salesman overpowering a customer, but simply and naturally in the course of their daily living.

In this book I have continually maintained that youth must choose their own values. No one can force another to value. But wise parents and teachers can expose young people to the kinds of experiences that will stimulate their moral thinking—that will facilitate value development. And the right kind of models can make the very best values look so attractive that these youth will want to build them into their own value systems. May God help us to be that kind of model. May God help us to respond to the cry of the younger generation, "Show me the way!"

Notes

[1] May, *Man's Search for Himself,* p. 241.
[2] *Ibid.,* pp. 244, 245.
[3] *Ibid.,* p. 204.
[4] White, *The Adventist Home,* p. 426.
[5] *Ibid.,* pp. 195, 196.
[6] *Ibid.,* p. 198.
[7] ———, *The Desire of Ages,* p. 353.
[8] ———, *Education,* p. 79.

Bibliography

Acock, Alan C., and Vern L. Bengtson. "On the Relative Influence of Mothers and Fathers: A Covariance Analysis of Political and Religious Socialization." *Journal of Marriage and the Family* 40 (August, 1978): 519-530.

———. "Socialization and Attribution Processes: Actual versus Perceived Similarity Among Parents and Youth." *Journal of Marriage and the Family* 42 (August, 1980): 501-515.

Aldous, Joan, and Reuben Hill. "Social Cohesion, Lineage Type, and Intergenerational Transmission." *Social Forces* 43 (May, 1965): 471-482.

Allen, Russell O., and Bernard Spilka. "Committed and Consensual Religion: A Specification of Religion-Prejudice Relationships." *Journal for the Scientific Study of Religion* 6 (Fall, 1967): 191-206.

Allport, Gordon W. *Personaity and Social Encounter.* Boston: Beacon Press, 1960.

———. "The Religious Context of Prejudice." *Journal for the Scientific Study of Religion* 5 (Fall, 1966): 447-457.

Allport, Gordon W., Philip E. Vernon, and Gardner Lindzey. *Manual: Study of Values.* Boston: Houghton Mifflin Company, 1970.

Arcus, Margaret Edwards. "Value Reasoning: An Approach to Values Education." *Family Relations* 29 (April, 1980): 163-171.

Argent, Russell H. "Compassion: The Heartbeat of Christian Education." *The Journal of Adventist Education* 45 (April-May, 1983): 5-7, 46, 47.

Aronson, Elliot. *The Social Animal.* 2d ed. San Francisco: W.H. Freeman and Co., 1976.

Beech, R.P., and A. Schoeppe. "Development of Value Systems in Adolescents." *Developmental Psychology* 10 (September, 1974): 644-656.

Bengtson, Vern L. "Generation and Family Effects in Value Socialization." *American Sociological Review* 40 (June, 1975): 358-371.

Brayer, Herbert, and Zella Cleary. *Valuing in the Family: A Workshop Guide for Parents.* San Diego: Pennant Press, 1972.

Counts, George S. *Education and the Foundations of Human Freedom.* Pittsburgh: University of Pittsburgh Press, 1962.

Dudley, Margaret. "A Study of the Transmission of Religious Values From Parents to Adolescents." Project Report. Heritage Room, James White Library, Andrews University, 1984.

Dudley, Roger L. *Why Teenagers Reject Religion and What to Do About It.* Washington, D.C.: Review and Herald Publishing Association, 1978.

Elder, Glen H., Jr. "Parental Power Legitimation and Its Effect on the Adolescent." *Sociometry* 26 (March, 1963): 50-65.

Faulkner, Joseph E., and Gordon F. DeJong. "Religiosity in 5-D: An Empirical Analysis." *Social Forces* 45 (December, 1966): 246-254.

Feather, Norman T. "Values in Adolescence." In Joseph Adelson, ed. *Handbook of Adolescent Psychology.* New York: John Wiley and Sons, 1980.

Flacks, Richard. "The Liberated Generation: Exploration of the Roots of Student Protest." *Journal of Social Issues* 23 (July, 1967): 52-75.

Fraenkel, Jack R. *How to Teach About Values.* Englewood Cliffs, N.J.: Prentice-Hall, 1977.

Frankl, Viktor. *From Death Camp to Existentialism.* Boston: Beacon Press, 1959.

Gardner, John W. *Self-renewal.* New York: Harper and Row,

1963.

Glaser, Barbara, and Howard Kirschenbaum. "Using Values Clarification in Counseling Settings." *The Personnel and Guidance Journal* 58 (May, 1980): 569-574.

Glock, Charles Y. "On the Study of Religious Commitment." *Religious Education.* Research Supplement. 57 (July-August, 1962): 98-110.

Hartshorne, Hugh, and Mark May. *Studies in the Nature of Character,* 2 vols. New York: Macmillan Company, 1928, 1929.

Hoffman, Martin L. "Moral Development." In *Carmichael's Manual of Child Psychology.* 3d ed. New York: John Wiley and Sons, 1970.

Hoge, Dean R., et al. "Adolescent Religious Socialization: A Study of Goal Priorities According to Parents and Religious Educators." *Review of Religious Research* 23 (March, 1982): 226-304.

Hoge, Dean R., Gregory H. Petrillo, and Ella I. Smith. "Transmission of Religious and Social Values from Parents to Teenage Children." *Journal of Marriage and the Family* 44 (August, 1982): 569-580.

Johnson, Martin A. "Family Life and Religious Commitment." *Review of Religious Research* 14 (Spring, 1973): 144-150.

Jones, Jeff. "Comparing Notes on Obedience to Authority: Dean and Milgram." *APA Monitor,* January, 1978, pp. 5, 23.

Kalish, Richard, and Ann Johnson. "Value Similarities and Differences in Three Generations of Women." *Journal of Marriage and the Family* 34 (February, 1972): 49-54.

Keeley, Benjamin J. "Generations in Tension: Intergenerational Differences and Continuities in Religion and Religion-Related Behavior." *Review of Religious Research* 17 (Spring, 1976): 221-231.

Knight, George R. *Philosophy and Education.* Berrien Springs, Mich.: Andrews University Press, 1980.

Kohlberg, Lawrence. "Development of Moral Character and Moral Ideology." In Martin Hoffman and Lois

Hoffman, eds. *Review of Child Development Research.* New York: Russell Sage Foundation, 1964.

Kohlberg, Lawrence, and Elsa Wasserman. "The Cognitive-Developmental Approach and the Practicing Counselor." *The Personnel and Guidance Journal* 58 (May, 1980): 559-567.

Lohne, Alf. "Adventist Crowds Create Unique Problems in Romania." *Adventist Review,* Feb. 9, 1984, pp. 14, 15.

McCready, William C. "Faith of Our Fathers: A Study of the Process of Religious Socialization." Ph.D. dissertation, University of Illinois at Chicago Circle, 1972.

McLellan, David Daniel. "Values, Value Systems, and the Developmental Structure of Moral Judgment." M.A. thesis, Michigan State University, 1970.

May, Rollo. *Man's Search for Himself.* New York: W.W. Norton, 1953.

Milgram, Stanley. *Obedience to Authority: An Experimental View.* New York: Harper and Row, 1974.

Nelsen, Hart M. "Gender Differences in the Effects of Parental Discord on Preadolescent Religiousness." *Journal for the Scientific Study of Religion* 20 (December, 1981): 351-360.

Newcomb, Theodore, and George Svehla. "Intra-family Relationships in Attitude." *Sociometry* 1 (July-October, 1937): 180-205.

Payne, Sam, David A. Summers, and Thomas R. Stewart. "Value Differences Across Three Generations." *Sociometry* 36 (March, 1973): 20-30.

Peck, Robert F., et al. *The Psychology of Character Development.* New York: John Wiley and Sons, Inc., 1960.

Pierce, Ponchitta. "Pearl of Our Hearts." *Reader's Digest,* June, 1979, pp. 186-192.

Proctor, Derrick L. "Students' Perception of the High School Environment as Related to Moral Development." Ph.D. dissertation, Purdue University, 1975.

Putney, Snell, and Russell Middleton. "Rebellion, Conformity, and Parental Religious Ideologies." *Sociometry* 24 (June, 1961): 125-135.

Raths, Louis E., Merrill Harmin, and Sidney B. Simon. *Values and Teaching.* Columbus, Ohio: Charles E. Merrill, 1966.

Rokeach, Milton. *Beliefs, Attitudes, and Values.* San Francisco: Jossey-Bass, Inc., 1968.

———. "The H. Paul Douglass Lectures for 1969." *Review of Religious Research* 11 (Fall, 1969): 3-39.

———. "Long-range Experimental Modification of Values, Attitudes, and Behavior." *American Psychologist* 26 (May, 1971): 453-457.

Rokeach, Milton, and John F. Regan. "The Role of Values in the Counseling Situation." *The Personnel and Guidance Journal* 58 (May, 1980): 576-582.

Rosen, Bernard C. "Family Structure and Value Transmission." *Merrill-Palmer Quarterly* 10 (January, 1964): 59-76.

Scharf, Peter, William McCoy, and Diane Ross. *Growing Up Moral: Dilemmas for the Intermediate Grades.* Minneapolis: Winston Press, 1979.

Sell, Charles M. *Family Ministry: The Enrichment of Family Life Through the Church.* Grand Rapids, Mich.: Zondervan, 1981.

Simon, S. B., L. Howe, and H. Kirschenbaum. *Values Clarification: A Handbook of Practical Strategies for Teachers and Students.* New York: Hart, 1972.

Smith, Maury. *A Practical Guide to Value Clarification.* LaJolla, Calif.: University Associates, 1977.

Strommen, Merton P., et al. *A Study of Generations.* Minneapolis: Augsburg Publishing House, 1972.

Thomas, Darwin L., et al. *Family Socialization and the Adolescent.* Lexington, Mass.: D. C. Heath, 1974.

Troll, Lillian E., Bernice L. Neugarten, and Ruth J. Kraines. "Similarities in Values and Other Personality Characteristics in College Students and Their Parents." *Merrill-Palmer Quarterly* 15 (October, 1969): 323-336.

Weigert, Andrew J., and Darwin L. Thomas. "Socialization and Religiosity: A Cross-National Analysis of Catholic Adolescents." *Sociometry* 33 (September, 1970): 305-326.

White, Ellen G. *The Adventist Home.* Nashville: Southern

Publishing Association, 1952.

————. *Child Guidance*. Nashville: Southern Publishing Association, 1954.

————. *Christ's Object Lessons*. Washington, D.C.: Review and Herald Publishing Association, 1941.

————. *Counsels to Parents and Teachers*. Mountain View, Calif.: Pacific Press Publishing Association, 1943.

————. *The Desire of Ages*. Mountain View, Calif.: Pacific Press Publishing Association, 1940.

————. *Education*. Mountan View, Calif.: Pacific Press Publishing Association, 1952.

————. *Evangelism*. Washington, D.C.: Review and Herald Publishing Association, 1946.

————. *Fundamentals of Christian Education*. Nashville: Southern Publishing Association, 1923.

————. *Messages to Young People*. Nashville: Southern Publishing Association, 1930.

————. *The Ministry of Healing*. Mountain View, Calif.: Pacific Press Publishing Association, 1942.

————. *Patriarchs and Prophets*. Mountain View, Calif.: Pacific Press Publishing Association, 1913.

————. *Thoughts from the Mount of Blessing*. Mountain View, Calif.: Pacific Press Publishing Association, 1956.

Wieting, Stephen G. "An Examination of Intergenerational Patterns of Religious Belief and Practice." *Sociological Analysis* 36 (Summer, 1975): 137-149.